DATE DUE

World Class Communication

World Class Communication

How Great CEOs Win with the Public, Shareholders, Employees, and the Media

VIRGIL SCUDDER
with KEN SCUDDER

WILEY
John Wiley & Sons, Inc.

Published by John Wiley & Sons, Inc., Hoboken, New Jersey.
Published simultaneously in Canada.

For general information on our other products and services or for technical support, please contact our Customer Care Department within the United States at (800) 762-2974, outside the United States at (317) 572-3993 or fax (317) 572-4002.

Wiley also publishes its books in a variety of electronic formats. Some content that appears in print may not be available in electronic books. For more information about Wiley products, visit our web site at www.wiley.com.

Library of Congress Cataloging-in-Publication Data:

Scudder, Virgil, 1950-
World class communication : how great CEOs win with the public, shareholders, employees, and the media/Virgil Scudder with Ken Scudder.
p. cm.
Includes bibliographical references and index.
ISBN 978-1-118-23005-3 (cloth); ISBN 978-1-118-28697-5 (ebk);
ISBN 978-1-118-28302-8 (ebk); ISBN 978-1-118-28297-7 (ebk)
1. Communication in management. 2. Communication in organizations. 3. Public relations. I. Scudder, Ken. II. Title.
HD30.3.S39 2012
658.4'5—dc23

2012022660

Printed in the United States of America

10 9 8 7 6 5 4 3 2 1

To my family: Susan, Ken, Kat, Nicholas, and Ryann, who have supported and encouraged me every step of the way.

Contents

Foreword

For today's CEOs and, frankly, for anyone who aspires to a leadership role, strong communication skills are imperative. Businesses operate in an "always on" media environment, and there are multiple audiences that expect—and deserve—to hear from the person in the corner office. As CEO and "communicator-in-chief" of Kraft Foods, one of my most important responsibilities is speaking about our company to our employees, reporters, financial analysts, shareholders, politicians, nongovernmental officials, and many other diverse audiences who have an interest in our activities and our role in the world.

As the "face" of our company, my words are carefully scrutinized every time I speak, and they often live in perpetuity in cyberspace. But it's not only what I say that matters; it's also how I say it. A hesitation, the wrong tone, or even an unconscious gesture on my part can affect our stock price. And when I sometimes have difficult news to share, my ability to communicate clearly, truthfully, and confidently goes a long way to reassure my audience that we're on the right track.

With so much at stake, it's no wonder I take communication so seriously. That's where Virgil Scudder comes in. For years, he has capably advised my executive team and me. That expertise is now compiled in this thoughtful and instructive book.

With his background in broadcast journalism, Virgil drives home the power of simple, conversational language, and teaches how to deliver a message with clear, short, definitive, jargon-free statements. He counsels the use of simple stories that paint mental pictures and specific examples to back up assertions that might otherwise fall on skeptical ears.

Much of our corporate communication takes place with a remote listening audience. So Virgil has taught us how to use the pace, volume, and tenor of our voices to capture and maintain the attention of our listeners. With these techniques, our audience can hear the same passion they would otherwise see from our facial expressions and gestures, if they were in the same room.

The "Scudder Method" works. Whether you're a CEO or whether you support one, this timely book provides valuable instruction and real-world examples of how executives can communicate clearly, confidently, and memorably.

Irene B. Rosenfeld
Chairman and CEO, Kraft Foods Inc.

Preface

It's not easy being a CEO. In fact, A.G. Lafley, the long-time head of Procter & Gamble who now serves on many boards, estimates that the job of a CEO may be among the five most difficult in the world.

As hard as it is to get to the corner office, it's even harder to stay there. The average tenure of a CEO is 3½ years. Too many stumble because they don't communicate effectively enough with the wide range of audiences they must now reach and persuade.

What are the keys to success? Why do some CEOs succeed when others of seemingly comparable talent and work ethic fail?

Very often the difference is the ability to communicate effectively with diverse constituents. Many executives focus too narrowly on the financial side of their business and overlook the importance of communicating with their employees, the media, and the public.

It's been estimated that 90 percent of a CEO's job is communication. I've discussed this with CEOs of many large and small companies, and not one has strongly disagreed with that assessment. Here are some of the most important communication obligations the chief executive faces:

- Shareholders have to be convinced that the CEO has a workable plan for the long-term success of the company.
- Employees have to be motivated to be loyal and work hard.
- Various levels of government need to be convinced that the company is operating ethically and within the law.
- Social and environmental groups need to believe that the company is a responsible corporate citizen.
- Customers and consumers need to have confidence that the company's products and services are safe and reliable.

The list is almost endless.

The job is even more difficult today due to the current atmosphere of distrust of business. The simplest move, even a right one, can sometimes be criticized as cynical, evil, or worse.

Today's companies have to be nimble, and leaders need to communicate as never before. Competition is global, and change is constant. Constituents must be effectively engaged. Strategic plans have to be created, communicated, and executed successfully. This requires good communication.

Yet, recent studies have shown that 60 to 90 percent of company strategies are not executed or do not deliver the intended results. In addition, more than 70 percent of employees are not actively engaged in their organizations.

Clearly the communication tasks of the CEO are formidable. The simple fact is this: Most CEOs today are good communicators, but few are great ones. "Good" might not be good enough in this Information Age. The corner office is no longer a sanctuary; today's CEO lives in a fishbowl! All heads of big companies, like it or not, are now public figures.

It's not just the CEO who may be on constant display. Cell phone cameras can catch any executive, or even line employee, at any company at any time, and in virtually any kind of situation. Words spoken in these impromptu encounters can quickly go viral and become a threat to an individual's career and a company's reputation. Thus, the ability to communicate effectively in such situations becomes a critical part of an executive's repertoire.

For over 30 years, it's been my privilege to coach and counsel leaders of scores of organizations, ranging from small businesses and charities to some of the world's largest and most powerful corporations. This work has been done in 26 countries on 5 continents. These leaders and I have been through many memorable experiences together, ranging from great successes to bold headline crises. In each case there were important lessons to be learned by me and by the people who headed these organizations.

In this book, I've tried to capture these lessons and illustrate them with real-life examples drawn to a great extent from my own experience. Whether the reader is the head of a large company, a not-for-profit organization, or a small family business, the principles and examples outlined herein can lead to greater success and more job satisfaction.

To add perspective to my own observations, I conducted extensive interviews with a number of CEOs and other experts on executive communication. These are people I know and respect, people whose effective interaction with various audiences has been a significant contributor to their success and that of others. The purpose of this book is to outline the areas in which a business or organization leader needs to communicate and provide best practices for doing so. Each chapter concludes with a series of tips to show you specific areas that need to be considered in all aspects of CEO communication.

This book is not intended to be a textbook, though it might well serve as one. It was conceived as a practical guide to success for CEOs, those who wish to be CEOs, and people such as public relations and investor relations professionals who support them.

I hope all of them find it useful.

Acknowledgments

One of the great privileges of my career has been coaching and observing some of the best communicators in the business world over the past three decades. While I was usually in the position of "teaching" them, I also learned a great deal from them. In writing this book, I sought to use their expertise and observations to flesh out my own ideas, and in some cases again remind me of some things about executive communication that I may have overlooked, forgotten, or simply not known.

All that I interviewed were very generous in giving me their time and sharing their wisdom: CEOs like Irene Rosenfeld, Jim Kilts, Larry Merlo, Glenn Britt, Andrea Jung, Steve Caldeira, William Murray, Steve Orr, Kathleen Jaeger, Olof Persson, Robert Taubman, Art Thamboo, and Joe Almeida; top public relations professionals like Bob Pearson, Ellen Schulman, Jessie Hackes, and Eric Kraus; first-tier speechwriters like Steve Soltis, Dana Rubin, Jim Holtje, and Jeff Sheshol; and outstanding journalists like Joyce Rosenberg of the Associated Press. I also benefited from the wisdom and professionalism of exceptional investor relations professionals like Chris Jakubik and Barbara Baker. To all of them I express my deep gratitude.

Credit must also be given to Jeff Thompson and the late Bob Young, my colleagues at Carl Byoir & Associates and Hill & Knowlton from the late 1970s to 1990, two of the finest media training professionals who ever practiced the craft; and to Dick Kulp, the outstanding lead trainer at Virgil Scudder & Associates for the last 20 years. Their talent and creativity was invaluable in developing many of the concepts and techniques that are commonplace in the industry today.

I also want to thank the team at John Wiley & Sons, especially Sheck Cho and Stacey Rivera, for their professionalism and endless patience as they helped guide a first-time book writer through the process. Among other things, I had to learn the difference between writing columns and articles and writing a book.

Most of all, I owe a great debt to my son, Ken Scudder. He and I started Virgil Scudder & Associates in the teeth of a recession in 1990, and the business has lasted 22 years through economic ups and downs. Ken is a superb manager, writer, and editor who deservedly shares name credit with me on the cover. It was Ken who made sure that I stayed on track and stayed focused during the many months of the process.

Great support also came from my wife, Susan, and the Los Angeles Scudders: my daughter Kathryn (Kat) Scudder, and my grandchildren, eight-year-old Nicholas and six-year-old Ryann. It was Ryann who kept saying to me on the phone, as only a little girl can, "When are you going to finish writing that silly book so you can come out here and see us?"

Soon, sweetheart, soon. You're quite a motivator.

PART I

The Essentials of Successful Communication

CHAPTER 1

The Scudder Method

"You can have brilliant ideas, but if you can't get them across, your ideas won't get you anywhere."

—Lee Iacocca, former CEO of Chrysler

What is communication?

Most people would give you a pretty quick, standard answer: "Communication is what one person tells another," or "communication is an exchange between people or groups of people," or even "communication is an exchange of data of one kind or another."

Here's what I think: communication is not what the speaker knows—to a large extent, it's not even what he or she says. Communication is what the listener takes away and what happens as a result of that takeaway.

You can liken it to teaching. Education is not what the teacher knows; it's what the student learns. The teacher carefully designs a lesson plan to reach each student with the most important message points on the subject.

The teacher provides us an excellent model for executive communication. Successful communication is based on understanding the listener, tailoring the message to the listener's interests and knowledge, and delivering the message in such a way that the most important points stick in the mind.

A teacher's measurement of success is how well the students perform on exams. An executive's report card is less specific, but no less important—it's how well he or she can persuade or motivate.

I spent the early part of my career in broadcast news. I interviewed scores of business leaders and witnessed interviews of far more. I also watched a lot of them in public speaking situations.

I often wondered why so many of these executives weren't better communicators. After all, these were accomplished people who had gone very far in their chosen fields.

Too many got trapped on interview questions that they should have been prepared for. They sometimes stumbled and fumbled around for answers. Many failed to tell an interesting or credible story. In public-speaking situations, it was not uncommon to see them bury their heads in their script and drone on for what seemed like an eternity, slogging through material that was of little interest to the audience.

After I left ABC News and entered the burgeoning media training field, I found out why they weren't better: very few executives made communication a priority. Thus, they dedicated too little time to honing their skills. Many would spend a lot of time improving their golf game but little or none on becoming better communicators. And all too often, they weren't sure where to begin to upgrade their skills.

Almost immediately after I became a media trainer, I found myself assigned to coaching leaders of some of the world's great companies. How could I give them a winning formula for every communication challenge they might encounter?

The answer was a system that became known as The Scudder Method.™

The Key Elements

The Scudder Method derives from my background in journalism. Journalists are storytellers. Almost all are good communicators. So I based the system on the way journalists, both print and broadcast, make news stories interesting and meaningful to their audiences.

It involves simplification, clarification, and illustration.

CEOs have to communicate with a lot of constituents and in a lot of ways. But the key to success in all of their venues is based on what I refer to as the four Cs. What is said must be:

1. Clear
2. Concise
3. Credible
4. Delivered with Confidence

I found ready agreement on this point from two CEOs whose communication skills have served them well. Time Warner Cable's Glenn Britt put it this way: "You need to have simple ideas, and consistently stick to them over a period of time." Former Gillette CEO Jim Kilts noted, "You have to be clear on what you're telling people. You've got to tell them over and over again, and make it simple, and illustrate it with pictures."

Pictures are a critical element of good communication because people remember pictures better than words. But Kilts was not referring just to photographs, drawings, or charts. He was also talking about word pictures—examples that stick in the mind and cause people to remember the points being discussed.

Here's where the journalist's model comes in.

The Communication Funnel

To show executives how to tell a complicated story briefly, as a reporter must often do, my firm created the communication funnel.

Print journalists take a large amount of information and boil it down to a cohesive news story. So do the best newsmakers, using these steps.

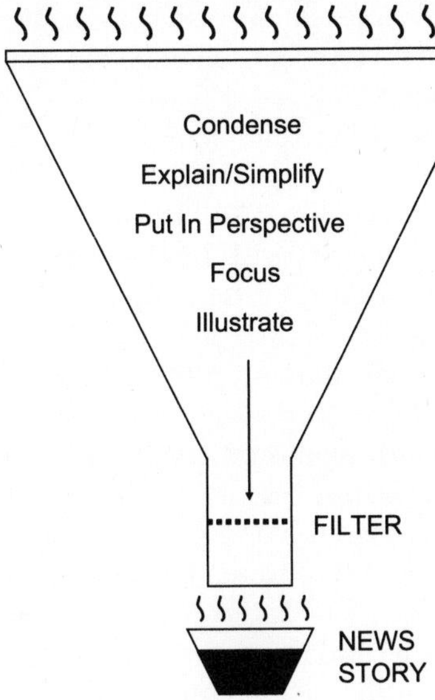

News Funnel Chart

It's simple, it's effective, and it should be the starting point for all executive communication. The following elements compose the funnel:

- **Condense.** A well-versed person starts with more material than can possibly be included in any one talk or interview. So cutting it down is the first step.
- **Focus.** The best way to trim the excess material is to focus on three headline points that cover the key messages. These should be the three sentences you want the audience to take away. The test is this: if someone who heard your speech or interview was asked, "What did he say," these three sentences are what you want the answer to be.

- **Explain.** This refers to both specifics and generalities. Any technical term or other reference that might be unclear should be briefly explained, and the reason or purpose behind what you are saying should be made clear to the audience. If you are taking an action, you should be able to answer the question "Why?"
- **Simplify.** Don't assume too much knowledge on the part of your audience, especially about your organization or company. One of the biggest traps CEOs fall into is assuming everyone knows as much about their work as they do. Also, boil complex words and ideas down to simple but still accurate and meaningful concepts.
- **Put points in perspective.** Provide any relevant facts that enable the audience to judge the importance of a point. As with the point about simplification, you cannot assume that your audience knows the surrounding facts or situation for what you're saying. Tell them why what you are saying is important.
- **Illustrate.** Use word pictures (examples) to make your points memorable.

Here's how it might work in real life. Let's say a reporter from *The Los Angeles Times* is sent to cover a speech by the governor of California. The speech might begin with a history of California commerce and transportation and run on for 45 minutes. Worse, it could be full of complexities and detail. But the reporter is allocated only a few paragraphs in the newspaper to tell the story.

Here's how the journalist would proceed:

The first step is to condense because there are a lot more words and ideas going into the funnel than the newspaper would ever be interested in printing or that people would care to read. Condense how? By focusing on three key points.

The writer will pick the theme, or most important point, to lead the story, and perhaps provide the headline for it (i.e., "Governor Calls High-Speed Rail Essential").

The next step would be to elaborate on the headline statement with three key points, such as:

1. The state's highways are choked with traffic.
2. The airports are badly overburdened.
3. The governor believes the new system will have great economic benefits and stimulate growth.

Those are clear points, easily understood by everybody.

But the governor or his engineering or financial experts may have gotten too technical in laying out the proposal for the system. The next step comes under the heading of "explain, simplify, or put in perspective." This could involve briefly gleaning key points from a complicated engineer's report or a detailed financial analysis and bottom-lining what they mean to taxpayers and travelers.

The final step is to illustrate. In this instance, that could mean providing visual examples. They could include word pictures about being stuck in traffic jams on Interstate Highway 5 or projected overcrowding conditions at San Francisco International Airport. The reporter could also use pictures of traffic jams, a map of the planned route of the railroad, or a chart showing how California's airports rank against the rest of the country in terms of delayed flights and traffic.

So the reporter has taken a long and perhaps dry speech and turned it into an interesting and clearly understandable article.

You, as a leader, should follow exactly the same process when preparing for a talk, a meeting, or a news interview: condense the facts and data to a few key points on which to focus; be sure they are properly explained, kept simple, and put in perspective; and, where possible, give examples or otherwise illustrate your remarks to solidify your points and make them memorable.

Another problem in telling a company's or industry's story is that some executives have the habit of speaking in sentences that are too long and complex. Many speechwriters fall into the same trap. At the end of such a long, complex sentence, listeners often forget where it began and what the point was.

The traditional 5-minute radio newscast provides a good model for tightening up sentence structure. The writer has to compress 10 to 12 stories into a framework of 3 to 4 minutes (allowing time for commercials), and each must be complete in itself. Because this is oral communication, sentences must be short, direct, and complete. The audience has no chance to go back and revisit material once it's spoken, unlike print where the reader can simply backtrack and read the sentence again.

Here's a good exercise for you: take the last speech you delivered and try to write a news story about it in six short paragraphs, just as the print journalist did in the California example cited earlier. It's a good discipline exercise and a step on the road to clear, succinct, effective communication. If you find you can't do it, the focus of your talk probably wasn't clear enough.

Once you've done that, pull out the three key headline points that you wanted people to take away from that speech. Now you've got the basis for any news interviews or any subsequent conversations on the subject. Did you have any news interviews after that speech and, if so, did your three points come clearly through?

Here's the supreme test: the next time you deliver a speech or do an interview, ask someone who was not familiar with your planning beforehand what your three key points were. If yours and theirs don't jibe, you have work to do.

To see if you're really at the top of your game as someone who can boil down detailed material to its essence, write a three-sentence radio news story about it.

For an example, let's go back to the high-speed rail story. Here's what a short radio report might look like:

> *Governor Jerry Brown told the California legislature today that the high-speed rail system is essential to the state's continued economic growth. Citing traffic-clogged highways, heavy air pollution, and overburdened airports, he called for immediate passage of a proposed $200 billion funding bill. The legislature is expected to vote on the measure next week.*

Headline-Elaborate-Detail

The Scudder Method also applies to how newsmakers should respond to questions. Our system is called Headline-Elaborate-Detail.

We use a simple inverted pyramid chart to illustrate how this works.

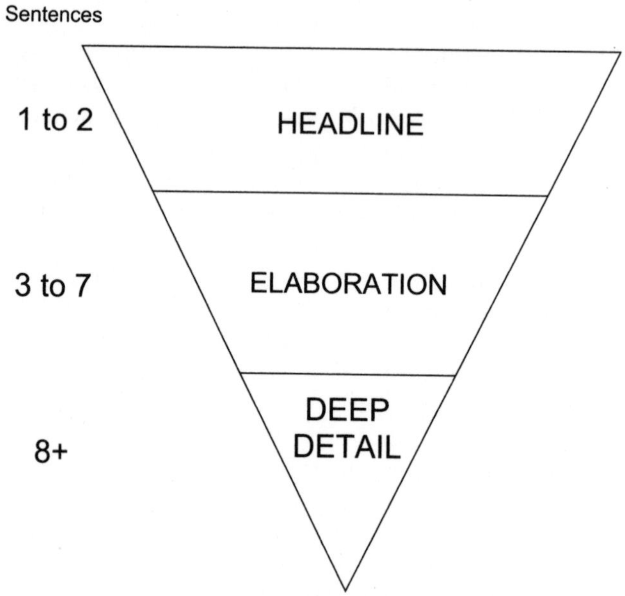

Satisfaction Chart

We regard a headline as one sentence, or occasionally two. The elaboration should run roughly three to seven sentences. We consider anything above eight sentences as deep detail.

Here's how the system works. When answering a question, the speaker should go into only the level of detail he or she feels necessary to fully tell the story, and the story should be encapsulated in the first three sentences. That sets the stage for what is to follow.

The headline should be the main point, the line that needs to be remembered if nothing else is. It presents the premise, or argument, on the topic.

This direct-to-the-point system is especially important in media interviews.

Because most television and radio news inserts run under 10 seconds these days, the headline point has to come first, followed with enough elaboration and detail to help the journalist put the story in perspective.

Using the high-speed rail example, when asked why he is calling for the high-speed rail passage now, the governor might respond, "This system is vital to California. It affects our health, well-being, and the continuing growth of our economy. We are choking on an outdated transportation system."

I timed my reading of those words at nine seconds, easily the right length to fit into any newscast.

In addition to providing broadcast journalists with a nice, tight news clip, he has given the print journalist three possible headlines or leads to the story: "Governor Calls Rail System Vital," "Governor Says Rail System Affects Health and Economy," and "We're Choking on Outdated Transportation, Says Governor."

He could go on to provide some detail that would help the journalist in writing the story, but the top line response to the interviewer's question has to be direct, simple, to the point. And, most of all, brief.

While we used a news story as our example, this system is effective in any kind of communication situation. Shareholders want clear, straight, bottom-line first answers and unambiguous comments; so do employees and government officials.

The Path to Being a Great Communicator

In summary, the Scudder Method is the key to becoming a world-class communicator. Never forget the lesson that began this chapter: communication is not what you know, or what you say; it's what the other person takes away. Tailor all of your oral communication accordingly.

This book alone won't make you a great communicator. That takes time, dedication, a willingness to look objectively at your own skills and abilities, some outside perspective, and practice, practice, practice. But using the techniques I outline will get you started down the right path. After that, it's up to you.

Tips

- If you want to be a world-class communicator, you have to dedicate the time and energy to improve.
- Think like a journalist when you create your messages.
- Be sure everything you say meets the "four Cs" standard.
- Whether a speech or interview is a long one or a short one, build it around a headline theme and three basic supporting points.
- Keep the sentences short and the words simple and understandable by everyone.
- Be sure to focus, explain, simplify, illustrate, and put in perspective.
- Use examples to make your points memorable.

CHAPTER 2

You Are a Brand: Make It the Right One

"A brand is a living entity. It is enriched or undermined cumulatively over time—the product of a thousand small gestures."
—Michael Eisner, former CEO of Walt Disney Company

As I mentioned earlier, a CEO's tenure is often very short—on average just 3.5 years. Some step down voluntarily but, in my experience, most of the people who occupy the corner office for a short time don't leave of their own choosing.

Sometimes the leader's departure is related as much to his or her image as to the company's P&L (which, itself, is affected by the CEO's image). And the image is very closely tied to the person's communication skills.

A brand is not built overnight. Every executive on the way up should be conscious of his or her brand and take steps to build one that is positive. If, for example, the executive is a caring person by nature, playing an active role in an important charity for the underprivileged would be a good way to use that aspect of the person's character to build his or her brand.

Brand damage, especially when compounded by poor performance or poor relations with a board of directors, can be fatal. Just think of Mark Hurd, who had to step down as CEO of Hewlett-Packard following discovery of inappropriate conduct, including expense account violations, in an investigation of a sexual harassment charge.

Hurd's resignation statement said it all: "I did not live up to the standards of trust, respect, and integrity that I have espoused at HP." That kind of a CEO image is very damaging to a company trying to convince its shareholders and customers that it operates by high standards.

Image = Brand

The CEO's image is his or her brand. Making and maintaining a positive CEO brand is critical to the success of the company. It must be managed and communicated.

Bob Pearson, whose career includes heading a prominent New York public relations agency and being the top PR aide to Dell Chairman and CEO Michael Dell, sees it this way: "A CEO, particularly a long-term CEO, really is a brand. You have to think of them in that manner. For example, you only take on speeches or public appearances that add long-term value to that brand."

Does every CEO in fact have a brand? Here's a test for you. Think of six CEOs, and assign each a one- to three-word definition from this list:

- Competent
- Arrogant
- Strong
- Sensitive
- Decisive
- Heartless
- Ineffective
- Underachiever
- Visionary

You see, you found the words that fit each. You just identified the image of each of the six. That's the brand.

A positive perception of the CEO greatly enhances the reputation and success of an organization. Studies have shown that companies that have a CEO who is well known and well regarded perform better in the stock market.

Let's look at a couple of high-profile executives from recent years: Jack Welch and Lee Iacocca. Welch is generally perceived as a smart guy who gets things done, even if a few people get trampled in the process. Iacocca has a somewhat gentler image but is still seen as a strong leader who can manage through the toughest times. In each case, their brands served them well in terms of the person's style and what he wished to accomplish.

What comes to mind when you hear the name Bill Gates? Genius, innovator, creator of a great and innovative company, but one known for hardball tactics on the competitive front. But there is yet another image that immediately comes to my mind, and perhaps yours, and it softens the latter: The Bill and Melinda Gates Foundation.

The good works of this substantial charity give a new dimension to the Gates image, that of a caring individual. The inclusion of his wife, Melinda, in the name and in the organization's activities further reinforces the picture of this businessman's humane side.

Real estate mogul Donald Trump has cultivated quite a different brand. His is a calculated, in-your-face approach—brash and demanding. He wants to be seen as a smart, tough guy. He loves publicity, and this image has enabled him to get tons of it. In fact, he gets publicity out of all proportion to competitors who may have as much to offer, or more, and who may produce a better return on investments. Referring to other business executives who criticize him for all of the TV attention he seeks and gets, Trump once told a public relations conference in New York, "They're just jealous."

Massive ego and self-promotion are wrong for most CEOs, but Trump has managed to make that less-than-lovable image symbolic of his demanding standards in terms of the high quality of his properties. And in a field where visibility is king, no one's residential properties in the United States have a higher recognition level than Trump's. However, his image would be absolutely wrong for heads of most companies.

Finding the Right Brand for You

What is the proper image, or brand, for a CEO? There is no one answer. What's right for the head of a company like Facebook would be wrong for the leader of a major law firm. But here are some of the things I've heard most frequently mentioned by investors, employees, and the public: strong, innovative, honest, and humble.

It's amazing how often "humble" was used in these conversations, especially by CEOs, and how many people from all of these discussions stressed that the worst image an executive could project was that of "Superman." The executive who takes all the credit when things go well can expect most of the blame when they don't.

Many things go into making a CEO brand. The list includes personal presence, dress and grooming, public appearances, philanthropic activities, and off-duty pursuits. All must fit the image of who the person wants to be and should not be removed from who the person really is.

The CEO's Presence

A key part of an executive's brand is "presence." Presence is hard to define, but as a U.S. Supreme Court justice once said about pornography, you know it when you see it. There are people who can walk into a room and command it without saying a word. Others could be in the center of the room for an hour and pass unnoticed. Something as simple as walking with a slouch can detract from a leader's presence.

U.S. Presidents Reagan and Clinton were noteworthy in their ability to command a room. I've heard old Washington hands say that when you were around one of them, you knew you were in the presence of the president of the United States. Some of the other chief executives of the last few decades, such as George W. Bush and Jimmy Carter, did not project the same aura.

What is the difference? Erect posture is part of it. So is eye contact, a friendly smile, a firm handshake, and a well-paced, well-modulated voice. Every one of these characteristics contributes to the sense that the executive has himself or herself, along with the situation, under control. The aura of leadership that presence conveys is invaluable.

Speaking too fast is a common fault of younger executives and even younger CEOs, particularly entrepreneurs involved in start-ups. This habit not only diminishes a person's presence but also saps credibility.

Some people have a head start in the presence game because they have a high level of self-confidence, but others can acquire a compelling presence through working on the things I just mentioned.

Here's how you can do a personal presence check. The next time you make a speech, ask someone to shoot a video of you walking up to the lectern and saying the first few words. You'll get a pretty good indication of your presence quotient by reviewing the video, and you'll know what to work on.

Your Look

Dress and grooming are also important to a leader's image. When women began to rise to high-level corporate positions in the 1980s, many went out and bought lines of clothing that basically copied men's attire—dressy shirt or blouse, long necktie, and a men's suit-type jacket. In my view, the message it sent was entirely wrong. It basically said a woman had to dress like a man, and perhaps think and act like a man, to be considered a good executive. It became a conspicuous copy of male attire, and it made the critical mistake of calling attention to itself. Clothing that calls attention to itself is almost always wrong; it should quietly enhance the image of the wearer.

Fortunately, the trend didn't last long. If you look at the average woman CEO today, you'll see someone who is very well dressed and whose attire is feminine but definitely says "business."

Clothing sends a message. Apple's late CEO Steve Jobs would never have thought of showing up for a presentation in a business suit; jeans are the common attire of the tech community. Similarly, you won't see Lloyd Blankfein of Goldman Sachs walking into a meeting wearing jeans. That's just not how it's done in the world of investment banking.

Public Appearances

Public appearances are also important to building and maintaining the brand, but they have to be in the right venues and align with both the brand and the priorities of the corporate executive.

The PR head of a large media company once complained to me that "our chairman, a genuinely nice guy, will agree to appear on virtually any panel with any other speaker if someone asks him to. That sends a wrong message. He ought to be limiting his appearances to prestigious international forums like the Davos economic summit. By appearing on lower level panels, he sends the message that our company is less important than it really is." I wholly agree.

It is essential that the head of a corporation be a limited edition, not only because the person's time is so scarce but also to indicate that this person and this organization are special. That means choosing and accepting only a few media appearances or speeches in any given year. Well-run companies often plan such appearances far in advance, spacing them properly for effect and timeliness in terms of what will be going on in the company or the industry.

A CEO's brand is significantly enhanced by appearances in key thought leadership forums. In the United States, that list includes the Conference Board, the Detroit Economic Club, Town Hall Los Angeles, the National Press Club, the Economic Club of Chicago, and the World Affairs Council of Philadelphia. Prime international venues include the World Economic Forum in Davos, TED International, and the Clinton Global Initiative. One appearance before such a group sends the message that this person is a respected business leader and the company is in good hands.

Similarly, media appearances must be carefully chosen. Leaders of large companies can command interviews with the likes of *The Wall Street Journal*, *The New York Times*, *Fortune*, CNBC, and Fox Business News, and that's where the emphasis should be. However, in my view, it would be a mistake not to occasionally sit, perhaps once a year, for an interview with the dominant newspaper in the headquarters' town. The favorable impact the resulting story can have on local residents, government officials, and the employees of the company is quite valuable. It is also likely to result in kinder, gentler treatment at the hands of the newspaper and other local media when times get bad.

Philanthropy and Your Brand

Philanthropic and recreational pursuits also affect the image of the individual and the quality of the brand. The right philanthropic involvement sends a message of both caring and leadership, but such activity needs to align with the interests of the individual and the goals of the company.

The best example may be The Bill and Melinda Gates Foundation, which I mentioned earlier. Microsoft's reputation was one of a company that wanted to rule the world. By focusing on international well-being and health, the charity played positively on that image, emphasizing the international aspects of the company but still helping soften the image of both Microsoft and Bill Gates.

The subject of philanthropy is covered in more detail in Chapter 19, "The Role of Philanthropy."

Public Behavior Affects Your Brand

In November 2008, the heads of the Big 3 automakers badly damaged their personal brands and became the butt of TV jokes when they went to Washington to seek money to bail out their troubled companies. Pictures showed them each arriving in their private jets, and those images stirred outrage from hard-pressed taxpayers. When the Big 3 leaders made a follow-up trip, they each traveled in one of their company's SUVs. Perhaps no one told them that there is good, nonstop commercial air service between Detroit and Washington with an abundance of first-class seats.

The world we live in today is one of instant communication with lasting effects. For a leader, privacy is a relic of history. Because today's cellular telephones have a video component, anyone is subject to showing up on an Internet video at any time. So what is believed to be private behavior can quickly become public behavior.

I remember an instance, prior to today's widespread prevalence of video-equipped cell phones, when a PR professional of a small but highly visible insurance company complained to me that her CEO and other top managers loved to visit strip clubs. While that is legal, public awareness of it would hardly create confidence in the maturity and responsibility of the CEO and his team. Today, a video of that management team coming out of such an establishment would quickly go viral, doing significant damage to the company and possibly ending the CEO's reign.

An old saying goes "[n]ever say anything you wouldn't want to read on the front page of *The Wall Street Journal*." I'd update that to "[n]ever do anything in public that you don't want whisked around the world on the Internet."

The public exposure risk from cell phone cameras is not confined to the Internet. Whereas television stations and networks once accepted only high-quality video, no matter how good the story, times have changed. If the story is important enough, they will often take whatever video they can get. Just think how many times you've seen blurry or grainy videos on television in stories where no broadcast-quality cameras happened to be on scene. Even interviews via Skype now show up on major television stations when the reporter wants an on-camera interview and can't get it otherwise.

Just as it is true that inappropriate action can damage an image, a lack of action can also be a negative. I once told the president of a high-profile company in a midsize southern city that I thought his firm needed a more positive image in its headquarters' town. I mentioned that he was not really involved in community activities. He responded indignantly, "I beg your pardon! I'm a member of the yacht club." That really wasn't what I had in mind.

Your Internal Brand and Investor Image

Internal brand building can be as important as the image projected to the outside world. Today's CEO needs to be seen by employees as the leader of a team, not the supreme commander in the corner office. That means projecting an image of openness and willingness to listen to subordinates. Familiarity with the executive in this case builds trust and loyalty.

Business has much to learn in this regard from the military. America's armed services place a high premium on good public relations, both internally and externally. A retired Army colonel recently told me that Army officers are taught to mingle with the troops, and generals walk the halls in the Pentagon, greeting everyone they see. This is a very good policy that many CEOs should adopt.

Skillful handling of shareholder meetings and investor earnings calls are also important to CEO brand building. It's a good idea to rehearse important investor meetings on video to polish the presentations and see just what kind of impression the executive team is making. Such rehearsals should also include intensive rounds of Q&A so that good impressions made in the initial presentation are not undermined by poor handling of questions.

Shareholder earnings calls are especially important to building and maintaining the CEO brand. The tone should be positive and straightforward. Because these events are audiocast, not videocast, the sound of the voice is critical. The aura of solid leadership must be conveyed by good presentation techniques. Keep in mind that the audio is likely to be posted on the company's website, so a good or bad performance will be out there for months to come. Too few CEOs go back and listen to these calls afterward. If they did, they would be more aware of how their delivery and handling of questions could be improved.

So ask yourself this about building your brand: What are my best personal features that I want to showcase? What actions can I take, and in what activities should I engage, that will result in brand building and brand recognition? What actions should I avoid, on or off the job, that could damage my brand? How can I best align my personal brand with the image I seek for my company?

The next time you see a CEO on television, ask yourself this: "What is his or her brand?" I'll bet you'll have an answer.

Tips

- Developing and enhancing the CEO's brand must be a priority.
- That brand has to fit the individual's personality and the mission of the company.
- Reinforce the brand through appropriate public appearances.
- Take the time to properly rehearse both public appearances and shareholder earnings calls.
- Check out your "presence" on video and work to refine it.
- Choose the right off-the-clock activities, and stay away from those that could send a negative message.
- Think humble, not Superman.

CHAPTER 3

Active Listening: A Critical Management Tool

"Listening can well be the difference between profit and loss, between success and failure, between a long career and a short one."
— Bernard Ferrari, author and consultant

Most CEOs are pretty good at talking. But some are not good enough at listening.

I noted earlier that many CEOs and outside experts agree that communication is 90 percent of a CEO's job, but *communication* does not mean just talking; it also means listening.

GE CEO Jeffrey Immelt puts it this way: "Listening may be the single most undervalued and underdeveloped business skill, especially in an era of increased uncertainty and fast-paced change."

Asking the Right Questions

"Most human beings harbor a huge misconception," says Andrew Sobel, author of *Power Questions: Build Relationships, Win New Business; and Influence Others.*[1] "It goes like this: If we could get some straight answers, we'd know the right decisions to make. The real truth is different: If we just asked the right questions, we'd understand what the real issues are, and the answers would come quite easily. We'd then know what to do—and what *not* to do."

Ask almost any CEO if he or she is a good listener and the answer you'll likely get is "of course. It's one of my strengths," and it will be said with great conviction.

But it's not always so. The CEO of a fast-growing craft beer company once told me, "One thing I'm pleased about is that we have a happy, loyal team." His head of public relations took me aside later and said, "Don't you believe it. Some of us are so frustrated at his top-down management style that we are about ready to quit."

Sobel says, "Questions are almost always more powerful and provocative than statements or direct advice—which most people don't take anyway. That's because they help us arrive at our own answers. We're more likely to embrace the answers we arrive at on our own than those someone dictates to us."

Bernard Ferrari, author of *Power Listening: Mastering the Most Critical Business Skill of All*, claims that many people *think* they listen when they really don't.[2] He says, "Listening means active involvement in a conversation. It means really absorbing what the other person is saying, not just sitting there nodding your head."

His recommendation follows the famous "80/20 Rule": the leader of a conversation should spend 80 percent of the time listening and 20 percent talking.

Listening to Advisors

Not everyone listens to the right people, or enough people, before making a decision. Some leaders will listen mostly to lawyers, some to bankers or buddies, and some to the last person who speaks. Wise management listens to all relevant parties but pays particular attention to input from the company's best listening post—the head of corporate communications—when an issue or policy can in any way affect the organization's reputation. No one can give better advice on how various constituencies will respond to a given action or, if uncertain, know how to find the answers.

Heads of corporations get bombarded with advice. How should a leader decide which people to listen to?

With a chuckle, former Gillette CEO Jim Kilts told me, "That's what they pay you the big bucks for." Then, in a serious tone, he added, "As a general manager, you get good at it over the years. And if you're not sure, you bring in experts."

Kilts says two of the biggest mistakes CEOs make, especially early in their tenures, are "thinking they need to have all the answers, and not picking, and listening to, good outside advisors." That doesn't mean, however, that you should ignore the people down the hall in your own company. Internally, he believes that staff meetings and town halls are essential for getting the proper input, along with one-on-one meetings with key executives.

We all think we listen. But do we listen in the right way? Do we too often listen for what we *want* to hear instead of what we *need* to hear?

"Listening is not passive," says Ferrari, a long-time McKinsey consultant. "You have to ask the right questions and guide the conversation."

Once the questions are asked, effective listening involves processing the information, assessing its reliability, checking it against other sources, and taking appropriate action.

The Price of Not Listening

Recent U.S. history is littered with examples of organizations that paid a high price for failing to listen to the right people or enough people, or to ask the right questions. They include MF Global, Susan G. Komen for the Cure, BP, Netflix, Bank of America, and Pennsylvania State University. All ended up facing serious reputation and financial damage (in one case fatal), because some person, or persons, didn't listen to a key voice and take proper action.

For four months, federal regulators told MF Global CEO Jon Corzine that he was taking excessive risks in buying up sovereign debt in countries like Greece, Italy, and Spain. But Corzine, convinced that the European Community would soon bail out these economies in a manner that would net his company a bonanza, barreled ahead. The former Goldman Sachs trader's big gamble ended up sinking the company.

The leadership of Susan G. Komen for the Cure ignored the advice of staff members when it cut off breast cancer screening funding for Planned Parenthood. The move, apparently the result of intense pressure from right-wing groups that opposed the fact that Planned Parenthood also provides abortion services, resulted in the loss of millions of dollars in contributions and a severe blow to its reputation.

BP apparently didn't listen to competent PR professionals when it mishandled media interviews in the wake of the Deepwater Horizon disaster. Some of the interviews worsened the already bad image the blowout and spill had caused the company. Statements by BP's leaders gave the impression that the company was unconcerned about the deaths and economic damage it had caused. (The negative image resulting from CEO Tony Hayward's comments is further discussed in Chapter 24, "Government Hearings: Don't Be Nervous. Don't Be Flustered. Be Prepared.")

The leadership of Netflix totally misread how customers would react when it suddenly raised its prices 60 percent and turned each member's account into two separate accounts: one for movies streamed via the Internet, another for DVDs sent by mail. Netflix members were surprised and angered by both moves. The result was a mass exodus: 800,000 customers fled in a single quarter, and the company's revenues and stock plunged. Apparently, no one asked any customers how they would react to the moves before Netflix pulled the trigger.

Bank of America made the same mistake when it suddenly slapped a $5.00 monthly fee on its debit cards. The result was mountains of bad press and expressions of outrage on social media, followed by a major drop in customers, and finally an embarrassing reversal of the policy. The ongoing impact of the move is even worse: every time a news story appears about questionable bank policies or customer practices, you'll likely find Bank of America somewhere in the story.

Even major universities are not immune to tuning out bad news and paying a heavy price for it. Penn State officials, including its director of athletics, head football coach, and university president, apparently "didn't want to hear it" when allegations began surfacing in the mid- to late 1990s that an assistant football coach was sexually assaulting young boys (even on university property). Had the right questions been asked, such as "What is our obligation to the alleged victims," and "How do we meet our legal and moral obligations in this situation," and the right actions taken, the university could have been seen as a responsible, active responder to the crisis. Whatever bad news resulted would have lasted for a relatively short time and would have focused almost exclusively on the university's decisive action when it learned of possible wrongdoing. But that didn't happen, and 15 years or so later, the scandal severely damaged the university.

Listening failures are hardly new or limited to large organizations. I remember in the late 1980s during my days with Hill & Knowlton, the international public relations firm, when we were called in to help an advertising agency that was fast losing clients over a statement made in a trial.

One of the agency's two partners had suddenly left the small but highly successful firm and taken much of the staff with him. The remaining partner sued, and he testified in court that the departing partner's action had severely damaged the business. Unfortunately, his testimony was too strong; so strong, in fact, that it scared off much of the company's remaining business. His comments went something like this: "We're devastated by this action; we can't even get the phones answered."

Suppose that was your advertising agency of record and you read that story in *The New York Times*. It probably wouldn't be your agency for long.

I asked the CEO/partner why he had made such a damaging statement in court. He responded, "Because our lawyer said it was necessary to win the case." But the company didn't win the case, it lost key clients, and it went under not long afterward.

Yes, the CEO had listened, but to only one voice—a voice focused on a single objective: winning the lawsuit. Successful listening involves hearing all the appropriate voices, filtering the information, and then coming to a conclusion that takes into account the input of all relevant sources. I believe any head of marketing or public relations would have strongly objected to that awful statement being made in court. Accordingly, such people, or qualified outside public relations counsel, should have been allowed a chance to voice their concerns before plans for the testimony were finalized.

Voices from Inside Your Organization

One of the biggest complaints employees make about top management is "they don't know what I do, or what I need to do my job better, and the reason is they don't listen."

Without disputing the point, which I'm sure is often true, let's turn it around. Maybe top management doesn't ask for, or welcome, comment. Therefore, there may be nothing for them to listen to.

One of the nicest and most impressive CEOs I ever met was Arthur Schultz, who headed the Chicago-based advertising agency Foote, Cone & Belding in the 1980s. Schultz usually ate lunch in the company cafeteria. After standing in line to pay for his food, he would often seek out a table with employees he didn't already know, sometimes young people in lower-level jobs. He would sit down, smile, stick out his hand, and say, "Hi, I'm Art Schultz. Tell me about yourself and your work here."

The result was high recognition and loyalty by employees, who saw themselves as not just workers but as part of his team. He told me he also got a lot of useful information and insights that were valuable to him in making company decisions. Even if a leader makes a decision that is contrary to what an employee recommends, the employee appreciates being asked and is likely to be more committed as a result of being seen as part of the decision-making process.

As one example of a good listener, Bernard Ferrari cites Arne Duncan, the U.S. Secretary of Education. He says Duncan likes strong people around him who will challenge his thinking and reasoning. "If he's in a meeting, he makes sure everyone speaks," says Ferrari, "and he doesn't accept silence or complacency from anyone." Duncan's goal as a leader, according to Ferrari, is not to reach a common viewpoint; the goal is common action, not common thinking.

I can't think of a better example of how to build a loyal and dedicated team that will give its leader all of its best thinking. CEOs set the standards for a company in every way—culture, ethics, and practices. A CEO who listens and encourages listening is likely to find that practice making its way down the ranks, to the great benefit of the organization.

Goldman Sachs, which had no end of bad publicity during the recent financial crisis, got a sharp and unexpected blow one March morning in 2012 in *The New York Times*. Greg Smith, a senior-level manager in its London office, resigned, but not quietly. An op-ed article under his byline in the *Times* essentially accused the big investment banking firm of betraying its clients by putting its own bottom line ahead of their interests. Those are serious charges, and such a public airing of the man's views were suddenly on the front pages of business sections around the world. The company lost $2.15 billion in market value in a day.

I had to wonder: could this be the product of management not listening? Could it be that Smith had tried to voice these concerns to his superiors and not been encouraged to speak out? Or was he simply a publicity-seeking rogue who was wrong in his accusations?

It's hard for anyone on the outside to judge. However, it should be cause for introspection on the part of any company's leadership. "Are we encouraging open dialogue and interaction on the part of our employees; or do we simply set policy and require them to follow it?"

Listening Sets Your Corporate Culture

My job takes me to many corporate headquarters. I guess I am what could best be described as an "insider-outsider." When I am inside the company meeting rooms with top management, I am an "insider," helping them deal with some of their most contentious issues. But, when I walk up to the receptionist's desk, or walk down the halls alone, I am an "outsider;" because most employees don't know me. And, in that latter role, often without asking a single question, I can get a sense of the company's culture in minutes.

Is it a company that fosters a positive atmosphere, where people look forward to coming to work and feel free to offer ideas and suggestions? Or, is it one where they look straight ahead and just do the job as they are told?

That's a pretty important question, and as much as anything else, you can boil it down to this: management's willingness to listen.

As a journalist, I always enjoyed covering the antics of New York City's colorful congressman, and later mayor, Ed Koch. Koch was always asking, "How'm I doin'?" It's true that this man of no small ego sought an affirmation of his performance. But he also was a highly intelligent politician with an ear to the public's opinions. I always felt he would welcome an honest answer—at least in the right environment from the right people.

Talking, and Listening, to Yourself

Sometimes people fail to ask the right questions of themselves and thus don't come up with a workable answer.

Occupy Wall Street is a grassroots movement that captured a lot of media attention with demonstrations and sit-ins in major cities across the United States in late 2011. Protesters expressed dissatisfaction with the growing imbalance of wealth in the United States. They quickly exposed the economic disparity in this country, and politicians from both parties, unions, and corporate leaders were forced to discuss the issue for the first time in decades.

But, after this initial success, the movement lost momentum. Why? While the changing of the seasons was a factor (as columnist Howard Fineman said, "Protests are a summer sport"), the perceived lack of a specific message or goal was, in my view, the main reason.

This essentially leaderless group didn't ask itself the right questions: What exactly do we want? What changes will we demand to fix the problem?

Perhaps they should have studied the tactics of Mahatma Gandhi, who led India to independence and set the stage for civil rights movements around the world. Gandhi's philosophy was that demonstrations should always be targeted to overturning one law or policy or getting rid of one specific public official. Obviously, he had asked himself the key questions: what will best move us toward our goal, and how can we accomplish it?

The leaders of the Arab Spring, the 2011 series of uprisings that toppled long-standing governments in several Middle Eastern countries, had a clear objective: get rid of governments that had failed to deliver for their people. Unlike Occupy Wall Street, these protesters had a clear, specific objective, not just grievances.

But, think about this: what caused the uprisings in the first place? Very simply, it was the failure of long-entrenched governments to listen to their people and make the kind of changes that might have kept them in office.

The best CEO listeners and managers are often those who think outside the box, such as by calling other industry CEOs and asking, "What are you hearing? What are people talking about in your organization? What do your constituents complain about?"

These are the same CEOs who are likely to ask top managers, "What are you hearing from your people, or from our customers, or from others with whom you interact?"

A good CEO regularly asks the head of communications, "What are people saying about us, both internally and externally? What is the social media buzz?"

This is the same kind of leader that will close a group meeting or a one-on-one session by asking, "Is there anything we haven't covered or anything you'd like to say?" Sometimes the most useful comments of the day result from that question.

With such a CEO who believes in asking questions and listening for answers, a smart manager can get a leg up in the game by initiating that conversation with a line like, "Here's what I'm hearing from my team."

There is also a nonverbal aspect to listening. Good leaders are attuned to the other person's body language. A shift in the chair, a loss of eye contact, or a nervous fidget can indicate a person's discomfort with the direction of a conversation. A smart leader will notice this and perhaps say, "You're not comfortable with this, are you? Why not?" The answer can be more valuable than anything previously said in the meeting.

Hearing the Outside Voices

Sometimes the boss's ears can be opened with proper access to outside sources. I experienced this some years ago in Australia. A new CEO at a bank in Sydney believed that his customers were quite happy with the bank. That wasn't my sense or the sense of his PR staff, so the PR director persuaded him to schedule a focus group of customers and others to "confirm his feelings."

In a focus group, a company's executives sit behind a one-way glass and watch and listen as a skilled moderator asks a group of volunteers a wide variety of questions. Questions about the bank were discretely slipped in amidst others on various subjects, so the participants would not know the purpose of the session or that the bank had sponsored it.

Every time the topic got to this CEO's bank, the comments were overwhelmingly negative. After only a few minutes, he got up and said, "I've seen enough. Let's go fix it."

The point is that third-party input, whether from a consultant or a focus group, can be invaluable to a leader who has doubts about what he's hearing from down the hall.

Listening to Anonymous Voices

Today's electronic technology has opened up new ways to ask questions and listen, but don't invite questions if you're not prepared to listen and respond effectively. The head of a large manufacturing company, which was in a difficult turnaround situation, set up an "Ask the CEO" email system (he used his name, but I won't). Employees could email a question to him, and he would provide an answer. A good idea, if properly handled.

However, it was badly mishandled. One employee asked, "Why are our products given such low quality ratings by *Consumer Reports*?" He responded, "I've seen that report and I'm not happy with it." That response can best be described as a "blowoff" because it didn't address the issue. People have no trouble detecting, and resenting, a blowoff.

His answer should have been, "I don't agree with those findings, and here's why . . . " or "CR made some good points, and we are addressing every one of them. Our team is firmly focused on quality, and I think you'll see those ratings change before long."

I couldn't help feeling that he was not the one who actually wrote that unresponsive answer. Not long after, he was removed from the job, and this incident was cited on the front page of a major newspaper as an example of his poor communication skills.

Companies today live in a world full of litigation and regulation. Criminal wrongdoing by even a lower or midlevel official, unknown by top management, can bring a company to its knees.

However, very often some people know of the wrongdoing and hesitate to speak up. After all, what can you do if your boss is the offender or if you suspect illegal or improper activity in the organization and everybody tells management, "No problem"? There is an answer in today's technology.

Some companies are setting up whistleblower hotlines in which an employee can report such matters anonymously. The company can then follow up with a discrete investigation to ask the questions that should determine whether the accusations are true.

That hotline is a form of asking questions and listening, offering top management the opportunity to find answers that might not be forthcoming in a face-to-face interview.

In sum, there are many ways of listening and many useful information sources. The smart CEO will think about them all and come up with the right questions to the right people that will lead to the right answers.

Tips

- Make listening a key element of your management style.
- Ask questions and seek comment from a wide variety of sources.
- In a meeting, spend more time listening than talking.
- Send the message down the ranks that managers are also expected to be good listeners.
- Listen to what customers and other key audiences think before making a key policy change.

Notes

1. *Power Questions: Build Relationships, Win New Business; and Influence Others*, Hoboken, NJ: Wiley, 2012.
2. *Power Listening: Mastering the Most Critical Business Skill of All*, Portfolio Penguin, 2012.

CHAPTER 4

Customs, Culture, and Language Count: Engage Humbly

"Don't overlook the importance of worldwide thinking. A company that keeps its eye on Tom, Dick, and Harry is going to miss Pierre, Hans, and Yoshio."

—Al Reis, marketing guru

"How is your French coming along?" I asked the American executive in Geneva, Switzerland, where he had worked for five years.

"I haven't bothered to learn it," he told me. "Everybody here speaks English."

True, English is the language of business, and everybody I've met on several trips to Geneva does speak English. But in any part of the world, the local tongue is the language of courtesy. French is the official language in Geneva and, by a wide margin, the dominant one in that area of Switzerland.

If you're going to work in a country, I think it's a mistake not to be able to greet people and converse on at least an elementary level in their own language. Even somewhat clumsy use of it (my French, for example) can help build bridges.

Few people rise to the top of a global corporation today without some service in a country or region far from headquarters. The executive's performance there can be a determining factor in whether he or she gets to the top.

Even a brief public appearance is enhanced by some use of the local language. Several years ago I was a keynote speaker at the national conference of the Canadian Public Relations Society in Quebec City. That city is the heart of French Canada and has been described as "a French town dropped into North America."

While the delegates came from all over the country, Quebec was the host chapter, so it seemed appropriate to begin my talk with a greeting in French before moving on to English. All of the speakers did this with the exception of one from the United Kingdom. He opened his speech with, "I will not begin my remarks in French, as my colleagues have, because of a long-held conviction: no one should abuse any language other than his own." It was clever and it drew a laugh, but I still think he would have been better off to open in French.

Learn the Local Business Customs

While being able to use the dominant local language is an asset to the executive and the company, some understanding of the culture is essential. Obviously, this starts with the no-no's—what *not* to do or say. This input is best gotten from local associates, either natives of the country or people who have been stationed in that place for a long time.

Olof Persson, president and CEO of Sweden's Volvo Group, says cultural differences in various parts the world are substantial, and a successful CEO of a global company needs to be aware of them.

"In the U.S.," he notes, "you can have open and frank communication—straight to the point; whereas in Asia you approach issues in a more indirect way. You have to make sure that you take a softer approach. It's something you have to learn."

He continues, "In the U.S. or Europe, I can say 'I've looked at the results and this is not good enough. We need to do this, and this, and this.' In Asia, one must use a more humble tone."

A good study in the mastery of bridging cultures is Jose (better known as "Joe") Almeida, the CEO and chairman of Massachusetts-based Covidien plc, a leading global provider of health care products. Brazilian by birth, Almeida has worked in his home country as well as in the United Kingdom and United States.

Almeida says he found communication in the United Kingdom even more candid than in the United States. When he told his assistant that he wanted to play golf at a particular club near his home, she responded, 'You don't have the pedigree to join the club.' She was very, very polite, but she said it the way she meant it. In the United States, you would say, 'You probably want to try some place else; they're very exclusive and they're very difficult about getting new members,' or 'The membership is closed.'

Almeida tells another story of cultural differences. When he started working in Boston, after coming there from a position in Brazil, his boss pulled him into his office and said, "You've got to be able to say what you want without beating around the bush." Almeida added, "The culture I grew up in is one in which you do not address and confront people directly."

The lesson here is clear: success lies in knowing the difference.

Art Thamboo, managing director of the Kuala Lumpur-based PR firm Eric Pringle Associates, says the biggest mistake Westerners make in his region is a lack of understanding and appreciation of social norms. He notes, "Malaysians, like their Asian brethren, do not like to be pushed for an immediate response to a proposal. There is also an unwritten protocol in terms of forms of address and respect for elders, and most of all, a condescending, know-it-all attitude is a definite no-no."

He adds, "In Thailand, comments about the Thai Royal family are out. In Malaysia, it's important to take an affirmative approach and to express a point of view without degrading an opponent. Also, touching a Muslim on the head is unacceptable, along with pointing with your index finger and some gestures."

Your Company's Culture

Just as cultures differ from country to country, they also differ from company to company.

Cultures come down from the top in a company, not up from the bottom. The CEO sets the tone for how the organization will operate. If that person is open, accessible, ethical, and positive, those down the ranks are likely to be so as well. A CEO who manages by fear and intimidation will find that those qualities will pervade the organization.

A new CEO who came up through the ranks is going to understand a company's culture on the first day on the job. Someone hired from outside might not, and that can lead to problems.

So when you take over as CEO, one of your first decisions is whether you will keep the current corporate culture or establish your own. You probably already made that decision, subconsciously, when you accepted the job. You looked at the company and said, "This is working, this isn't working," and started a plan to implement your management style.

So how do you impart your idea of the company's culture through the organization? There are several methods.

As I mentioned a few paragraphs ago, the most direct way is through your own actions. Employees will look to you for clues on how you expect them to act. This is the canard about "leading by example." Whether they mean to or not, your employees, especially those working directly under you, will follow your lead on employee relations, dress, communication style, and even language use. This means you can't have an "off day." You must exemplify the culture you want your company to have every day, especially in those first few weeks and months on the job.

Should you tell people directly what you expect from them? Maybe. Internal documents saying "here is how I want you to act" can seem dictatorial (which I don't recommend as a good culture); however, a more subtle approach saying, "I encourage everyone to speak freely to me about whatever situation they come across," or "I'm looking forward to meeting with as many of you as possible to discuss our future and seek your input," can work wonders.

Even if you come into a new company and feel that the corporate culture needs to be changed, you have to be respectful and mindful of the old culture, especially if that company has been successful under the old culture.

There were various criticisms of Carly Fiorina's unsuccessful tenure as CEO of Hewlett-Packard. Many, of course, were related to bottom-line results and decisions on the directions the company should be taking.

Others, however, involved culture. There were complaints about her seeming lack of respect for the company's founders, William Hewlett and David Packard. She was also accused of alienating HP engineers and customers. The no-nonsense Fiorina might not have been a good fit for the cultural climate at HP.

Robert Nardelli flamed out at Home Depot in part because his autocratic management style ran contrary to the entrepreneurial culture that had made Home Depot number one in its field. His demeanor turned off employees and the public and alienated store managers who were critical to the success of the business.

Part of Home Depot's value proposition had been the ready availability of expert advice from seasoned professionals—plumbers, electricians, carpenters, and so on. But, Nardelli cut back on them in favor of less-experienced and less-expensive part-time people. Customers noticed, and many felt that what had been a reliable information source for do-it-yourselfers, as well as a place to get the tools and supplies they needed, had become just a well-stocked warehouse. Home Depot lost a key element of its culture. Meanwhile, rival Lowe's was fast expanding its network of stores with innovative ideas, broader merchandise offerings, and a pledge of service excellence. The end was in sight for Nardelli.

I saw cultural differences firsthand when a public relations agency that I worked for was bought by a larger one. The old agency was a relaxed, informal operation that was sort of in the style of the 1960s advertising agency portrayed in the TV series *Mad Men* (minus the drinking in the office). There was terrific *esprit de corps*, including many company parties that celebrated its achievements and its objectives. Colleagues often went out for drinks together after work, and more than a few good ideas for clients came out of those get-togethers. The atmosphere was positive and upbeat; it was an exciting place to work. Creativity blossomed all over the place.

The agency that acquired us had a different style altogether. It was a good agency that produced some fine work, but it was much more buttoned down than we were. Colleagues rarely got together after work, and company parties were virtually nonexistent. The level of camaraderie was much lower. I always had the sense that creativity suffered as a result.

An employee who could not adjust to the new culture was not likely to succeed there, and indeed, many good people soon left or were let go.

Any CEO new to the job should take a hard look at the company's culture. Does it motivate people to do their best work? Is it likely to lead to innovation or to just playing it safe? Does it make people want to work there? Does it have everyone feeling like part of a team?

In many cases, cultures will need to be changed, particularly if the CEO inherits a defeatist or excessively complacent atmosphere. I will touch on this in more detail in Chapter 21, "Crisis: A CEO's Supreme Test."

However, if you are going to change the culture, understand that some employees will resist. Why? For some, it will be because they think the old system worked well. But, for most, it will be just because they aren't used to doing things that way. Habits get ingrained easily, and changing them is difficult. While the culture you are installing in the company may be familiar to you, it could be foreign to your staff. Give them time, and let them learn the benefits of working "your way."

Of course, it is critical that you have one, consistent, culture. Several years ago I was called to Paris to conduct media training (separately) for the co-CEOs of a very large multinational European company. One was French and one was German. They had different personalities, different styles, and different outlooks. I wondered at the time how the company could possibly have a smooth and productive working environment under two such diverse power-sharing leaders. It wasn't too many years after that experience that a new, single CEO took the reins.

Regional Cultures

Just as nations and companies have varying cultures, so do regions of many countries. The smart communicator will recognize these differences and adjust accordingly. If you speak to a business executive from Milan and one from Rome, you'd think you were talking to people from two different countries. They will be likely to have very different outlooks on business and life.

New York is full of fast talkers—things move very quickly there. So do its people and, in many cases, their mouths. But fast talking is a turnoff in the Midwest and the South, so a New Yorker is well advised to slow down the pace a bit in those areas and leave any New York accent or local idiosyncrasies (standing "on" line, rather than "in" line, for example) at home. Similarly, a deep southern drawl and expressions such as "y'all" can make northerners feel (often wrongly) that the speaker is not cultured or educated. Some of my business friends in the South will laden their speech with "y'all's" at home but never when traveling.

Culture, both geographical and corporate, is one of the most overlooked aspects of business, yet it is one of the most important. The culture that you, as CEO, set for your company is paramount in how the company is seen, how its employees act, and how well it is able to do business.

Tips

- Take some time to understand the culture of the country in which you are working.
- Learn at least some of the native language.
- Respect their customs, titles, and institutions.
- Make strategic choices about your company's culture.
- Be sure your demeanor and actions represent the culture you want.
- Understand regional, as well as international, differences in culture.

CHAPTER 5

Where's the CCO?

"Public relations as a function of executive management is central to the success of the corporation."
—Portion of Arthur W. Page Society vision statement

Does your company have a CCO? If so, you may be the only one. If not, I think it's something you should consider.

I don't know of a single company that has a position called "Chief Communication Officer" (CCO), yet I believe every company should. It would be appropriate recognition of the importance of the role the PR leader plays. He or she should be part of the C-suite and report directly to the CEO.

C-level titles have exploded in recent years: Chief Information Officer, Chief Accounting Officer, Chief Marketing Officer, and so on. A lot of these didn't exist 10 to 20 years ago. Why not a CCO?

PR Must Report Directly to the CEO

In too many companies, the public relations head reports to departments such as marketing, human resources, or even legal. This limits that person's effectiveness. After working with public relations professionals and leaders of corporations for over 30 years, I do not believe that a CEO can be fully successful without a close and interactive relationship with a competent head of communications.

Some enlightened organizations do have the head of the public relations function in direct communication with the top officer today, but far too many do not.

The public relations director, or head of corporate communications as companies increasingly call the position, is the eyes and ears of the organization: the person who can best spot an opportunity for favorable publicity and act as the "canary in the coalmine," the person who can sense trouble before anyone else in the organization does.

Let's look more closely at an example of the latter. When the leadership of Susan G. Komen for the Cure cut off breast cancer screening funding for Planned Parenthood in an apparent surrender to right-wing pressure groups, a firestorm erupted that sent Komen reeling. The organization lost millions of dollars in contributions and sustained serious damage to a positive reputation that had been built over decades.

A competent public relations counselor, sitting as a C-level officer in the meeting in which the fateful decision was made, would likely have strongly warned against the move and perhaps gone so far as to offer a resignation if the policy was enacted.

There are numerous other examples in recent years in which organizations have found themselves in turbulent waters when input from the right CCO would have steered them away from trouble.

What Does Corporate Public Relations Do?

In too many companies, the role of public relations is misunderstood and undervalued. It is seen as a function of marketing, or a unit created only to grind out news releases, Facebook posts, or newsletters.

True, those are valid and useful public relations functions. But they are generally the responsibility of lower-paid specialists who handle them well. It is poor utilization of resources to have a competent head of public relations engaging in such chores.

The head of public relations should be seen as a counselor and strategist. But many who now have that relationship with the CEO have told me that they are hampered by their title and lack of executive conference room access in dealing with C-level executives.

A good example comes in the legal arena. While the situation is changing somewhat, many corporate lawyers still have a "just say 'no comment'" policy. The fact is that in legally sensitive matters, top management, lawyers, and PR experts need to work in concert, particularly if a company's reputation is at stake.

I have too often seen CEOs sit idly by while a corporate attorney, operating from good intentions but focused only on the legal arena, lays out a policy that damages a company's goodwill. The total impact on the company, not just the legal impact, needs to be taken into consideration.

For example, not to publicly answer charges that a company's products are unsafe simply because the matter is going to court is a very foolish policy. Business will undoubtedly suffer.

True, there are things that can't be said, and comments on the particular case must be very limited, but silence can be perceived as guilt. Ask yourself this question: when is the last time you heard a journalist say "The company refused to speak with us" and you thought, "Well, they're probably innocent"?

Lawyer Jodi A. Janacek discussed this in the February 2009 issue of *Young Lawyers* magazine. She claimed that in a high-profile case, with a high level of media attention, it might become necessary to bring public relations experts into the inner fold. She noted, "Advice from, and management of, the media by a public relations firm in certain instances might make a difference in maintaining a somewhat unbiased jury pool, settling, obtaining a favorable verdict, or minimizing the amount of damage."

"No comment" is never a good answer. Giving the public relations head a seat at the head table and a voice in the discussion would often prevent problems of public perception without damaging the legal case.

Working with Your Head of Communications

Eric Kraus, senior vice president of corporate communications and public affairs of Covidien, doesn't have the CCO title *per se*; but he enjoys what is most important—a close relationship with CEO Joe Almeida. Kraus puts it this way: "A direct line between the head of communications and the CEO is critical. The communication officer has to have that direct link and partnership to be able to capture the voice of the CEO and work with other direct reports on a peer-to-peer basis. You have to have a 'joined-at-the-hip' relationship or you're not going to have a strong corporate brand. It just doesn't work."

Olof Persson, the head of Volvo Group, the big Swedish manufacturer of trucks, buses, and construction equipment agrees, saying, "You need to build a trust between the two of you. You have to find someone who understands you as a person in order to find the right style, in order to find the right level, in order to prep you with the right data, and also make sure that they are one step ahead in thinking what might or might not happen."

If a person is to be given a C-level title and the authority that goes with it, it's essential that the right person be selected for the job. Just what should a CEO look for in filling this role?

- **Experience.** No one can properly handle this job without a significant background in dealing with a wide variety of corporate crises and opportunities. Part of the job is spotting reputation threats before they become full-blown and warning top management of the potential damage. In addition, the person needs to be able to properly advise the CEO and other top officials as to what media or public speaking opportunities are right for the company.

- **Business knowledge.** While the CCO does not have to have the managerial skills of the CEO or the financial acumen of the CFO, a solid knowledge of business and the current business climate is essential.
- **Strong people skills.** To be successful, this person must be both likable and persuasive. He or she will have to tell people things they don't want to hear and do it the right way. That can include advising another C-level officer that a proposed plan or statement could have terrible media repercussions, politely telling another that "no comment" will only cause the company more problems, or turning down a journalist's request for an interview with a high-level executive without alienating the journalist. Diplomacy is an essential skill in this position.
- **Respect as a professional.** This job requires building a bond with the most important journalists and media outlets. A person who is not respected by them will not be able to get management the opportunities the company needs or do damage control on negative stories.
- **The ability to stay calm under stress.** There is plenty of stress in a CCO's job, from both internal and external sources. The CCO must be able to handle it coolly and calmly and perform his or her responsibilities in the most trying times.

A recent incident in Vancouver, British Columbia, Canada, provides a vivid example of what the head of communications should *not* be. When Sara MacIntyre, the media handler of the premier of British Columbia tangled with reporters, she became the story, and in a very negative way. That's a cardinal sin in the profession—making the story about yourself and not the leader.

MacIntyre told reporters at a trade show that her boss would not be taking questions that day—they would merely have a photo op—even though the permier was standing just a few feet away talking to an exhibitor. When the journalists pressed further for just a few questions for the premier, the communications director became clearly irritated and argumentative. Chewing gum all the while, she rudely interrupted them in midsentence and walked away as they pursued her constantly repeating, "She's not taking questions today." The press aide never gave a reason why despite being asked repeatedly. Since the premier was heading back to the provincial capital of Victoria after the trade show, the reporters would have no further opportunity for an interview, sorely displeasing them and their editors.

Of course, this being the information age, a video camera was rolling, and soon the video of the testy PR person zipped across Canada and around the globe. Bad behavior videos quickly go viral these days. MacIntyre's demeanor became the story, rather than the premier's interest in the clean technology, which was the focus of the show she was touring. Canada's *Globe and Mail* called MacIntyre "TV's newest villain."

A sure-fire opportunity for positive media coverage was turned into a media disaster.

Principles of Good PR

The Arthur W. Page society, the premiere organization for heads of communications of large firms, provides some excellent guidelines for good public relations and for the people who engage in the profession. The principles of public relations management it stresses include:

- **Tell the truth.** Let the public know what is happening and provide an accurate picture of the company's character, ideals, and practices.
- **Listen to the customer.** Understand what the public wants and needs.
- **Manage for tomorrow.** Anticipate public reaction and eliminate practices that create difficulties.
- **Remain calm, patient, and good humored.** As spokesperson, your demeanor will be seen as the overall attitude of the company. Losing your cool does a disservice to everyone (except tabloid journalists).
- **Conduct public relations as if the whole company depends on it.** No corporate strategy should be implemented without considering its impact on the public.

Any CCO should be someone who believes in these principles and adheres to them.

Does a company need to have a person with the title of Chief Communications Officer? Perhaps not, if the person in the job has a direct line of communication with the CEO and is in the inner circle to provide advice when major decisions are being made.

However, in my view, the title resolves all doubt as to the critical importance of the function and the respect and authority the person in the position needs and deserves. I strongly recommend it.

Tips

- Regard the public relations department as the eyes and ears of your company.
- Establish a close and direct relationship with the head of your public relations unit.
- Consider establishing the position of Chief Communications Officer.
- Fill that position with an experienced person who is first and foremost a strategist.
- Be sure that person is briefed in advance before every major decision and given a chance to weigh in on what the public relations consequences might be.

CHAPTER 6

Words Matter

"How often misused words generate misleading thoughts."
—Herbert Spencer, English philosopher

Languages are full of nuances and contradictions. Often that is part of their beauty. But, words can have more than one meaning, and it's easy to send a wrong message through a poor choice of words.

The words of a CEO can carry hundreds of times the weight of anyone else in the company. The CEO is seen as the embodiment of the company, and anything he or she says can and will be used for or against the chief executive in the court of public opinion. This makes finding the right words in all situations of paramount importance.

As I said in Chapter 1, communication is what the audience takes away. That is why it's important for all speakers to think about the language they use from the audience's point of view.

For example, when an Englishman says he has a "scheme" for something, it's a positive. It means he has a plan. However, when an American refers to a "scheme," the meaning is generally negative. Yes, it's a plan all right, but it's an illegal, unethical, or sinister one.

"Strong" versus "Growing Stronger"

U.S. President Barack Obama gave a good demonstration of the awareness of subtle language differences in his State of the Union message in January 2012. He said, "The state of our union is growing stronger."

That sounded like the line most presidents use in a State of the Union address: "The state of our union is strong." But it wasn't.

Why the change from "strong" to "growing stronger?" Because everyone was aware that the nation faced many problems, especially a weak economy with a high rate of joblessness. "Strong" would have given his Republican detractors campaign ammunition—"the president doesn't understand the problems of ordinary Americans." But because the economy and the employment situation were slowly improving, he could make a case for "stronger," thus sounding somewhat optimistic while depriving his opposition the chance to use the statement against him.

I don't know this for a fact, but I would not be surprised if the president and his team had gone through several iterations of that phrase before choosing "growing stronger." I suspect they weighed the relative merits of "improving," "turning the corner," "better," and "strong," and then decided that "growing stronger" gave the right impression to the audience.

Lose the MBA Phrasebook

Too many business leaders thoughtlessly spout words and phrases from the MBA playbook without thinking about their impact or properly backing them up: "enhancing shareholder value," "pushing the envelope," "maximizing returns," and so on. These buzzwords are so overused and convoluted that many people just tune them out. They are also seen as crutches employed by people who are either parroting the latest "business speak" or are trying to cover up for the fact that they don't really know their subject.

Here are some of the most commonly used corporate jargon crutches: "low-hanging fruit," "incentivize" (try "motivate"), "outside the box," "circle back," and "learnings" (say "lessons.")

Why say "endeavor" when "try" means the same thing? "Begin" is a better word than "commence," "count" than "enumerate," and "carry out" or "start" beat "implement."

A current virus in the English language is "no problem" in response to "thank you." Why should a favor or service represent a problem or lack of one? "You're welcome" is still the right thing to say.

This line, which came from an email, may be the ultimate example of "business speak" excess: " . . . An end-to-end , fully-scalable, robust, cross-platform, user-friendly solution." A good editor might be inclined to jump off the building after reading that one.

A character on *The Simpsons* once asked his bosses, "Excuse me, but 'proactive' and 'paradigm'? Aren't these just buzzwords that dumb people use to sound important?" He was fired immediately, but he did have a point.

Don't for a minute assume that those words and phrases mean the same to everybody.

Larry Merlo, the chairman and CEO of the large pharmacy firm CVS/Caremark, says one word that he never uses in employee meetings is "productivity." "The minute you say that," he says, "employees begin to worry about job losses, when that may not be what you mean at all."

By focusing on how the audience will hear his words, Merlo has chosen not to use the wrong word. In the process, he has spared his employees a lot of anxiety and himself the hassle of working with a worried crew.

The Right Word Can Preempt Problems

Several years ago, I served as chair of the International Section of the Public Relations Society of America. I finished my term and moved on to other things. How should I, and other one-time leaders of the group, be referred to? "Former chair?" No. The organization uses the term *past chair*.

What's the difference? Plenty. The term *former chair*, while accurate, raises questions. Was he thrown out? Did he resign in disgrace? Lose an election?

Past chair sends a different message. It implies that the person served honorably and moved on. One word makes a big difference here in how the situation will be perceived.

The right choice of words can also help a leader avoid potentially embarrassing situations, such as being unable to quickly come up with someone's name. Both politicians and business executives meet a lot of people. Remembering all of their names is virtually impossible.

U.S. President Richard Nixon (1969–1974) had a solution that I've used since I first heard about it. If you don't recognize the individual, and there is any chance you have met previously, don't say, "It's good to meet you." Instead, say as Nixon did, "How nice to see you." That simple phrase can prevent a lot of embarrassment. Nobody is turned off by "How nice to see you."

A later candidate, Democrat Al Gore, learned that the hard way in his 2000 campaign for president. He was introduced to someone at a fund-raising event in his native state of Tennessee and said, "Great to meet you." To Gore's dismay, that person turned out to be a major fund-raiser whom he'd met with several times.

Phraseology can be very important. A CEO of a large consulting company once made a presentation to an investor group that went pretty well, until it got to the Q&A. Then he blurted out a random thought that rattled investors—"I wish I felt better about the pipeline." A better way to express the same thought would have been, "I am intensively focused on improving our pipeline." Same situation, different impact. The stock dropped.

A simple lesson here is that it's almost always better to phrase things in positive terms than in negative ones. When a news reporter asks, "What are your company's biggest problems,?" I like to see the executive respond with "Like any company in this economy, we face a number of challenges. But I believe they are all manageable. Here are the ones we'll be focusing on."

The Wrong Words Last a Lifetime

Ill-considered utterings have a long shelf life in this day of sound bites. It will be a long time before people forget or forgive a careless remark by then-BP CEO Tony Hayward in the wake of the April 2010 explosion and oil spill in the Gulf of Mexico. Hayward was trying to assure people that both he and BP very much wanted to get the spill cleaned up and the damage rectified as soon as possible. Unfortunately for him, he phrased it, "I'd like to get my life back."

The comment created an outpouring of criticism. It created the impression that he cared only about himself and not the people whose lives had been disrupted or lost through BP's actions. Because of this and other factors, he was out of a job within weeks.

Here's an example of how careful word choice can play out in an investor earnings call. To keep pace with costs and to increase profits, companies sometimes raise the prices of their products. There is nothing wrong with that in a competitive business environment, but it's a subject that has to be handled carefully.

Large consumer products companies that sell goods to retailers that then sell them to the public are always under pressure to cut their prices to retailers. When talking about price increases, these companies often use a standard line: "We took pricing to cover increased input costs and other expenses." The result is usually a chorus of yawns. However, if the statement says, "Our price increases helped improve our margins," some customers—the large retailers—are going to immediately be on the phone demanding price breaks to share the wealth.

On the assumption that both statements are true, emphasizing the cost angle puts the company in a better position in terms of dealing with both its customers and in a better light in the court of public opinion.

At This Point in Time . . .

If I hear those words one more time, I think I will scream. One thing that separates the good communicators from the bad ones is that the good ones shed such verbal crutches.

Simple, direct language is almost invariably the most elegant language, but certain words and phrases slip into the language and hang on to our dialogue like barnacles clinging to a ship.

The expression "at this point in time" apparently began in 1973 when a lawyer for the Nixon White House used it in testifying in the Watergate hearings, and subsequent speakers picked it up. It then found its way into the language. It's about time it found its way back out.

When I hear "at this point in time," my impression is that the speaker is trying to impress someone with his or her erudition, but it doesn't impress. It comes across as stiff and pretentious. Simple, common language is often not only the most eloquent, but invariably the most appreciated by the listener. Other meaningless or tired expressions that should be headed for the oral trash heap are "if you will," "at the end of the day," and "it's early days."

An executive's use of language gives a perception of who that person is. Language that is laden with long, complex words or trite, overused phrases creates a sense of distance between speaker and listener.

Why, in an earnings call, would you say "utilize" when you would say "use" to a family member? Those calls, and all other executive communication, should be phrased in common terms.

The wonderful BBC series *Yes, Minister* chronicles the battles between MP James Hacker and the head of his staff, Sir Humphrey Appleby. In the 1981 episode "Doing the Honours," Hacker proposes a change to England's system of awarding its various end-of-year awards. Appleby's response to the proposal (which he does not want to see implemented) is a terrific example of unclear language whose purpose is to muddy the issue and hide what he is really saying:

> ***Sir Humphrey Appleby:*** *And to that end, I recommend that we set up an interdepartmental committee with fairly broad terms of reference so that at the end of the day we'll be in the position to think through the various implications and arrive at a decision based on long-term considerations rather than rush prematurely into precipitate and possibly ill-conceived action which might well have unforeseen repercussions.*
>
> ***James Hacker:*** *You mean no.*

There are many other examples that I'm certain you can think of yourself. Always look for the simplest word or phrase that will express what you mean.

Something that I find jarring is the current ubiquitous use of "issues." It's become a catch-all for just about anything that is unresolved. Unfortunately, it has found its way into the common language and even in the columns of some of the best written and best edited newspapers. I would submit this: if your plant is suddenly down, you don't have an "issue." You have a "problem." If you are in a dispute with a local government unit as to whether you should be allowed to expand your facility, you have "issues."

When an official uses a crutch phrase frequently, it and he can become the butt of humor. A former U.S. president was extremely fond of saying, "Let me make it perfectly clear." Yes, it gave a signal that what was about to be said was important, but it also produced smiles and chuckles.

President Ronald Reagan, a strong communicator overall, used to start far too many responses to questions with "well." It stuck to him. Today, if you see the clue "Reagan sentence starter" in *The New York Times* crossword puzzle, the answer is "well."

Executive speech should sound fresh, warm, and friendly. Clichéd words and phrases, along with overused expressions, create a sense of distance between speaker and listener.

The Right Words in Another Language

As mentioned in the preface to this book, I've conducted training sessions in 26 countries on 5 continents. In most cases I was working with executives who, while English may not have been their native tongue, had a good working knowledge of the language, so I was able to get my message across. However, there are specific challenges whenever you head overseas in phrasing your message correctly.

Seldom do words matter more than when speaking to an audience for which your native tongue is their second or third language. In this situation, a number of rules must be carefully followed.

Short, familiar words, simple phrasing, and brief sentences are essential. So is speaking at a moderate pace. In addition, a very important and often difficult thing to do is to avoid idioms and idiomatic expressions.

Many a speaker has seen an audience sit in puzzled silence when an American says something like "It's fourth-and-goal for us." That may have a very clear meaning to a fan of American football, but it might puzzle someone in Bangalore.

I remember a headline on one of my first trips to London several years ago that was a classic puzzler for a foreigner: "Rain Queers Test Pitch." That headline was clear to a local sports fan, but I had to read into the story to figure out what it meant: a major athletic contest had been called off because of a soggy field.

I mentioned before how the same word can have different meanings to different people. I learned how true that is years ago when I was on one of my frequent trips to Australia. After a long training day I went for a drink with a colleague. The club we went to was having a drawing, and as I bought my ticket the waitress wished me good luck. I replied that I knew she'd be "rooting for me."

After she walked away, my colleague told me, "Virgil, 'rooting' means something very different in Australia." It turns out that, instead of meaning to pull for someone or a team to win, in Australia it means . . . well, let's say it refers to the physical act of love. Fortunately for me, the waitress took no offense. When I later apologized, she smiled and said, "I understood what you meant. We get a lot of Yanks in here." So think before you speak. Practice and evaluate what you're going to say, whether it be in the text of a speech, a media interview, or any other public appearance. Test out your language on your colleagues and team.

And keep reading. The meanings of words change over time—keep up with them.

Words matter. A lot. Choose them carefully.

Tips

- Use simple and commonly understood terms, especially when speaking to someone for whom your language is a second language.
- Be cognizant of words that can have more than one meaning.
- Avoid MBA-speak wherever possible.
- Always try to phrase things from a positive viewpoint rather than a negative one.
- Slow down your speaking pace if people in your audience are less than completely familiar with your language.

CHAPTER 7

Be Strong: Apologize

"Apology sends the clearest signal that we have the strength of character to reconcile ourselves with the truth."
— John Kador, author and communication consultant

"I'm sorry."

Two little words. Seven letters. Clear, simple English. But words that many leaders seem unwilling to speak. That can be a critical mistake.

John Kador, the best-selling author of *The Manager's Book of Questions*, calls apology "a critical skill for leaders to develop accountability."[1] In his book *Effective Apology*, Kador says apology is "a marker of confident leadership. It's the catalyst for restoring broken relationships and a pathway for personal growth."[2]

But some CEOs say, "I don't apologize; it's a sign of weakness."

They are wrong. Apologizing at the right time in the right way is, in fact, a sign of strength. It shows a level of confidence—it says you, as a leader, know that you have a body of work strong enough to survive making, and admitting to, a mistake.

Apology alone rarely solves problems. In addition to expressing sympathy or contrition, steps must be taken to right the wrong or correct the conditions that brought the problem.

Dangers of Not Apologizing

In my experience, both as a former news broadcaster and as a coach and consultant to top management, people tend to be very forgiving when leaders admit mistakes and act to rectify the wrong. But the apology must be timely, heartfelt, and straightforward.

Failure to apologize, and take remedial steps, has doomed more than one leader. It has even brought down a presidency. I have long believed that U.S. President Richard Nixon would have finished his term with honor, rather than being forced to resign in disgrace, had he followed the right course during the Watergate scandal.

Nixon's instincts, and perhaps a serious character flaw, caused him to make fatal mistakes when he learned of the burglaries that triggered the Watergate scandal. Rather than do the right thing, his immediate reaction was "we have to cover this up." It was the cover-up, not the burglaries, that destroyed his presidency.

What should he have done? He should have gone to the American public with this message: "Terrible things have been done by loyal people who wanted to secure my re-election. They have been fired, and will likely face charges. Even though I was not aware that these illegal acts were taking place, and did not authorize them, I accept responsibility for them as Commander in Chief. I want to apologize to the American people, and assure them that such acts will never be repeated on my watch."

Nixon had many great accomplishments during his presidency, including opening up China to the West, creating the Environmental Protection Agency, and cooling Cold War tensions with the Soviet Union. But, invariably, when the name Nixon comes up, the first and often only thing that comes to mind is Watergate. It didn't have to be that way.

Personal views can often keep an executive from issuing an apology when one is clearly in order. Several years ago, I was called in to advise a company that could not extricate itself from damaging front-page stories and critical columns in newspapers in its city and state. The firm, which was in a state-regulated industry, had a made a serious misstep. The organization had outed a gay state official who they believed had wrongly denied them state contracts.

The official sued, and a stream of bad headlines followed. My recommendation was to quickly settle the lawsuit and apologize to both the official and the public for this inappropriate intrusion into someone's private life. The chairman of this privately held company refused, saying that he would not apologize to a person he considered to be "immoral." As a result, the matter dragged on and on, and journalists had a field day with the story.

Years later, the lawsuit was settled, but for a much higher price than the original claim, and only after the chairman issued an apology.

One of the reasons CEOs sometimes refuse to apologize is advice from their lawyers that the result will be increased legal liability, but this is faulty thinking, according to Kador.

He cites, as an example, Toro, the maker of lawnmowers and snow blowers. Traditionally, when customers complained of being injured by one of its products, Toro's policy was "deny and defend." When Toro later switched to a more conciliatory policy, starting liability claim discussions with an apology, even when it felt the customer was wrong, the number and cost of lawsuits dropped dramatically.

More recently, we've seen Toyota lose its number one position in the auto industry in part because it did not immediately fix and apologize for dangerous manufacturing defects in its cars. BP's failure to immediately and effectively address and apologize for the April 2010 explosion and oil spill in the Gulf of Mexico was devastating to the company's reputation and its bottom line.

Apology cannot exist in a vacuum. It must be accompanied by an acknowledgment of what the problem was, what caused it, and what is being done about it. It must be timely. Remedial action must be taken. Apologizing without action only makes matters worse, leading to a never-ending string of stories, not only about the company's inaction but also its hypocrisy.

Who Should Hear Your Apology?

When is apology appropriate, and when is it the responsibility of the CEO?

Obviously, one size does not fit all here, but as a general rule, a company should apologize when its actions or inactions have harmed or inconvenienced any of its important constituents: the general public, customers, employees, and shareholders.

Keep this in mind, however: not all apologies have to be broadcast to the world or expressed by the CEO. The magnitude of the problem and its impact are key determinants for whether a CEO should apologize.

If, for example, a technical glitch causes a company's payroll checks to be delayed for a few days, an apology should be issued internally by the official in charge of payroll. But if an incident affects the general public, especially one that causes death or injury, and is due in whole or in part to some shortcoming on the part of the organization, the apology should be publicly and widely aired, and that apology should come from the CEO.

But suppose a serious incident occurs that the company could not avoid, such as a flood or an earthquake. If the company took all reasonable precautions before the incident and handled it well when it occurred, no apology is in order. Instead, the CEO needs to be out in front, praising those who responded effectively during the emergency such as employees, police, firefighters, or rescue workers, and thanking them for their service.

This should be accompanied by an assurance that all possible steps are being taken to bring things back to normal. These steps should be outlined in detail.

An apology is not appropriate when an incident is beyond an organization's control or before it is certain that the organization somehow bears responsibility for what happened. However, an expression of compassion and steps to help those killed or injured in an incident such as I just described is always in order.

What Should an Apology Include?

First of all, your apology should be and sound sincere. When right-wing radio commentator Rush Limbaugh apologized for calling 30-year-old Sandra Fluke a "slut" and a "prostitute" on the air because she was advocating for insurance coverage for contraceptives, many people doubted his sincerity and sponsors fled the program. He lost over 30 sponsors in a matter of days.

Few took his apology seriously for a number of reasons. First, his barrage of insults was not a one-time occurrence. He trashed Fluke, a law student at Georgetown University, on the air for three more days after the initial remark. He apologized only after he began losing sponsors. Worse, he tried to play the victim, saying he regretted "acting too much like the leftists who despise me."

Apologies made under duress, without the sense of a sincere *mea culpa*, ring hollow.

To be effective, an apology needs some explanation of how it happened ("I was trying to make a joke," or "I just lost my sense of judgment and fair play," etc.) and a promise that the same offense won't be repeated in the future.

There aren't many instances in which a business leader will need to publicly apologize, but when an apology from the leadership is necessary, the apology should be concise, sincere, and specific. Once this is done and action is taken, the healing can begin.

Tips

- Evaluate carefully when an apology is appropriate.
- Be sure the right person is making the apology.
- Be specific in what is being apologized for.
- Give some explanation as to how the harmful words or action(s) occurred.
- Don't apologize for something not under your control.

Notes

1. Kador, John. *The Manager's Book of Questions: 751 Great Interview Questions for Hiring the Best Person*, New York: McGraw-Hill, 1997.
2. Kador, John. *Effective Apology: Mending Fences, Building Bridges, and Restoring Trust*. San Francisco, Berrett-Koehler Publishers, Inc., 2009.

PART II

Vital Constituencies

CHAPTER 8

Investors: Handle with Care

"It is not the return on *my investment that I am concerned about; it is the return* of *my investment."*

—Will Rogers, American humorist

The investor relations game has changed dramatically in recent years. More people own stock, directly and indirectly, than ever before. The volume of trading has reached levels that few ever thought possible.

Stock pickers express their views in loud and colorful terms online and on television. Influential personalities like Jim Cramer do not hesitate to call for a CEO's head, and it seems they do so fairly often.

As I said in the beginning of this book, it's not an easy time to be a CEO. You face some tough audiences, often led by big investors relentlessly demanding ever-increasing margins. As long-time stock market analyst and writer William M. LeFevre once said, "There are only two emotions on Wall Street: fear and greed." That's a tough atmosphere to deal with.

The CEO of a publicly held company essentially has two sets of bosses—the shareholders and the board of directors. Either can sink the ship. When you add to that a Greek chorus of critics and second-guessers, the pressure can get pretty intense.

Credibility and Transparency Rule

Ask a CEO what his company's most valuable assets are and you'll get a variety of answers. Some will say, "Our brand," others respond, "Our people" (although they often don't mean it), and yet others will cite such things as their product line, innovation, or global reach.

But there is another one I would put at the top of the list: credibility. Credibility breeds trust, and trust is essential to the long-term success of any organization.

How is trust achieved? Primarily by truth-telling and transparency. Truth-telling includes laying out a company's story in clear, direct terms and not minimizing or hiding problems.

Investors are demanding transparency today as never before. Don Tapscott, coauthor of *The Naked Corporation*, says, "Greater transparency is an unstoppable force. It is the product of growing demands from everybody with an interest in any corporation—its stakeholder web—and of rapid technological change, above all the spread of the Internet, that makes it far easier for firms to supply information, and harder for them to keep secrets." Tapscott goes on to say, "Rather than engage in future resistance to it, firms should actively embrace transparency and rethink their values and generally get in better shape."

Transparency is not only an increasing requirement for companies; it is also good for the bottom line. Robert Eccles, author of *Building Public Trust: The Future of Corporate Reporting* and *The Value Reporting Revolution: Moving Beyond the Earnings Game*, says that companies with fuller disclosure win more trust from investors.[1] He contends that relevant and reliable information means less risk to investors and thus a lower cost of capital, which naturally translates into higher valuations. So companies that share the key metrics and performance indicators that investors consider important have more value than those companies that keep information to themselves.

Transparency is not important to investors alone. In their 2008 book *Transparency: Creating a Culture of Candor*, authors Warren Bennis, Daniel Goleman, James O'Toole, and Patricia Ward Biederman described transparency as "the free flow of information within an organization and between the organization and its many stakeholders, including the public."[2]

There is another factor, however, that is often overlooked, and that also has great bearing on a company's credibility: clarity. It's the first element of our four-point system for telling the company's story in all investor forums:

1. Clear
2. Concise
3. Credible
4. Delivered with Confidence

Quarterly Earnings Calls

Nowhere is this standard more important than in the quarterly earnings call. While such a call may be one of top management's least favorite rituals, it's a fixture in today's business world. You can't escape it, and it needs to create the right perception of the company.

In real time, these calls last about 60 minutes. In "cybertime," they last for months or years. Both audio and video are commonly posted on company websites and elsewhere, easily accessible at no charge to anyone who wants to look or hear, so more than ever, a strong performance on your earnings call is a corporate necessity.

Too often, a call is a dull recitation of numbers without meaning, but when done right, it's an effective affirmation of a company's progress and the quality of its management.

There is one basic question on every call: Is the management fully aware of whatever situation(s) it faces, and does it have a viable plan to deal with it (or them)?

Good calls bolster investor confidence in the management and the organization's prospects for future growth and profitability. A badly handled call, even one with no negative surprises, can sometimes cause a drop in the stock price.

I became aware of this several years ago when I read a story in *The Wall Street Journal* about an industrial company suffering a 2 percent stock drop after a particularly bad earnings call. "There was no news," said one analyst, explaining that investors, who were already becoming less sold on the company's management, were reacting to the seemingly lackluster approach to the call and the business.

Should a CEO participate in this exercise every quarter? Most do, but not all.

One of the factors to be considered is who owns the company. If the stock is mostly held by large institutional investors, the CEO's presence is less important because they will have plenty of access to him or her anyway. But if the shareholder base includes a lot of smaller retail investors or a mixed base, the CEO should be on every call.

One time that the CEO absolutely should be on the call is when bad news has to be delivered. It's essential that the top person spells out the problem, the reason, and the remedy, tells what he or she is doing about it, and faces the questions that will follow. That is a definition of leadership.

If you ask most CEOs who listens to earnings calls, you'll likely get a look of surprise at such a seemingly obvious question, followed by the quick answer, "Investors, of course." True, they are the primary audience, but they are only part of the picture. Also among the audience may be employees, media, unions, customers, government officials, and suppliers. All have an interest in what the company is doing, and their reactions can have an impact on the company's fortunes. So a lot of potential listeners have to be taken into account in developing the messaging.

Here's a simple example. A unionized company that is reporting record profits and paying big dividends and bonuses will perk up the ears of its union leaders, especially around contract renewal time. Life will be easier on the management if such announcements are accompanied by a statement of plans to plow back a significant portion of the earnings into research and development or stock buyback.

There are CEOs who feel that an earnings call is merely a report of numbers. I disagree. I think it is a statement of where the company is and where it is going. That statement has to be carefully crafted.

Preparing for the Call

What is the path to a successful call? Obviously, all earnings calls begin with the gathering of the relevant numbers and developments. Once that is done, the intense work begins.

For most companies, I recommend two days of final preparation for the call, preferably the two days immediately preceding it. While different companies prefer to approach the process in different ways, following is my system for preparation.

The first day begins with an examination of the quarter's results. All key players need to participate—CEO, CFO, the head of investor relations, a public relations staff member, perhaps a member of the legal department, and the outside consultant (when one is used). It is assumed that a preliminary opening script and news release will have been drafted prior to this session.

I use Post-it-type wall sheets to lead a discussion of what will be emphasized during the call and what challenges the participants might face. We begin by identifying the three or four key positives and negatives of the quarter. The positives will be turned into points that will be stressed in the opening statement, the Q&A, and the news release that is sent out on the day of the call.

The key negatives may or may not be included in the script, depending on their severity. Significant bad news should be addressed in the script, both for reasons of transparency and to lay the foundation for the discussion of it, getting management's perspective in first. But all negatives will get extra attention in the preparation for the Q&A portion of the call, and specific answers to each of them will be developed and placed on the "Negatives" sheet.

Next, we select the three or four key points to be stressed for each division, product line, or geography and put them on separate wall sheets. Here are some examples of what these sheets might look like, starting with the positives and negatives.

Key positives

- Strong sales and revenue growth—each up double digits
- New product launches beat expectations by 10 percent
- Cost containment program beginning to produce results, with $50 million in savings

Major negatives

- Margins are still below our forecasts.
  - Slow but steady improvement last three quarters
  - Cost containment program will improve this
- We continue to lose market share on three major brands.
  - New sales initiatives starting this quarter
  - Advertising increases in select markets
  - Still have three of top seven brands
  - Two brands gaining share
- Inventory reduction program is not producing the anticipated results.
  - Long-term process
  - Getting some results, but working to improve
  - "Turning a battleship"

Now let's look at sample geography sheet, using Brazil as an example:

- Sales continue to grow double digits.
- We are increasing our presence in key retail outlets in major cities.
- Our cost-cutting measures are starting to take hold.

And now to product categories, using a video game as an example:

- While initial sales were slow, our new game is picking up momentum.
- We will double our advertising and promotional investment in this product in the next quarter.
- We remain confident that it will achieve our projections for the year.

These wall charts have a number of purposes. Being the combined work product of the entire team, they represent the best thinking and insights of the key players. They form the basis of a re-examination of the earnings call script and the accompanying news release. And, not least, they can be left on the wall for the call's Q&A period, so the management can quickly spot the key points and respond instantly and convincingly to questions.

The next step is to make any appropriate script or news release revisions. Once this is done, each call participant should read through the script aloud, with the support team listening and looking for any clumsy language, word echoes, or inaccuracies. A straight read-through also allows for timing the presentation. Most calls are scheduled for an hour, and I recommend that the upfront scripted session run only about 20 to 25 minutes to give the analysts on the call adequate time to ask questions.

If the company uses PowerPoint on the call (something I generally recommend, especially for the CFO's portion), this also should be reviewed for editing and updating at this time.

Once the desired revisions are made, each participant should again deliver the script aloud. This time it should be audio recorded and played back and critiqued by the speech consultant. A confident and authoritative delivery is essential to success in these calls because the executive is only seen and not heard. Poor delivery often translates as poor or uncertain management.

The Q&A

Now it's time to focus on the Q&A portion of the call. The team should collaborate on identifying all likely questions and coming up with three or four bullet point answers for each, on which the top management can elaborate.

By day 2, things should be pretty well refined and ready for final dress rehearsal. Once again, each call participant should deliver his or her opening segment aloud, and it should be audio-recorded for playback and critiquing. This allows for fine-tuning the delivery and a final check on the clarity and impact of the message.

Then the Q&A rehearsal begins. The supporting team fires questions at the call participants, who then respond (hopefully in line with the points agreed upon in the planning phases). More than one company has run into serious problems when a CEO or CFO ventured from the game plan and began spewing out random thoughts on key topics.

Here's an example from real life. The CEO-designate of a major financial institution was asked on an earnings call about his plans for a potential merger. The answer, taken from a transcript of the call, may or may not have been delivered with confidence, but it certainly did not meet the standard of clear, concise, and credible. As you'll see, he had not prepared for that predictable question:

> *Forgetting the business logic and the price, there will be options down the road there, I would answer your question about capable and that we really weren't quite capable yet because our army was doing all the other stuff we had to do, particularly the systems conversions. The army will be capable to do other stuff sometime next year, which is reasonable. Doesn't mean we will.*

I guess this was a long-winded version of "not now."

This man, who went on to become a successful CEO at the company, was not off to a good start. In addition to puzzling the analysts on the call, he ended up being featured in a *New York Times* story entitled "When CEOs Are Entangled in Their Own Web of Words." (Business section story by Landon Thomas, Jr., November 9, 2005.)

Around the same time period, another CEO boasted that a recent acquisition could produce as much as $80 million in cost savings for his company.

But this is what he said when asked to give more detail on that forecast:

I'll try to answer you, but you can't put a lot of faith in what I'm going to say. I know in one meeting I said if we look at this a year from now it will be clear, or should be clear, you, what is and what we can do and what's attainable and how quickly, and I still think that's true. God knows, I would only hope that's true.

Not very reassuring, is it? The company's stock, which had risen sharply when the deal was announced, dropped 8 percent that day.

He probably should have responded, "I still think it's true, but time will tell. Here's how we're working to make that happen."

If a company's executives prepare properly, the kind of confidence-sapping responses cited here should never happen.

For credibility, responses to questions should be "headline first," as outlined in Chapter 1, "The Scudder Method." When asked if a company plans a stock buyback in the coming quarter, some will respond, "As you know, market conditions are in flux. There are various other ways to employ our free cash flow. We would have to consider a lot of factors, etc."

A better answer is simply this: "That's uncertain at this time. It will depend on a number of factors, including timing and price. However, our buyback plan for the year remains unchanged." Get to the point and elaborate only to the degree that you need to. The degree of elaboration on a question should be determined by how much the company wants to say about the subject, not whether the answer is well-planned and organized.

As in the opening presentation, the Q&A rehearsal should be audio-recorded and carefully reviewed on playback. Answers that may feel good when spoken can sound anything but good when you hear them played back. A second or third take is often necessary to make the process as smooth and consistent as it needs to be. This fine-tuning of Q&A is one of the most important elements of a successful call.

This kind of best-practices approach to earnings call preparation does require time and commitment on the part of management, but the price of a bad call is too great to consider neglecting this process.

Writing the Opening

A good presentation must always begin with a good script. There is no way even the best executive communicator can effectively deliver a bad opening script. The writer must avoid such frequent mistakes as sentences that are too long or complicated, words that are unpronounceable or arcane, or trite MBA-like phrases or references.

A script should begin with a CEO's characterizing statement that puts a headline on the quarter and sets the tone for the material that is to follow. Here is one example: "This was another solid quarter for Z Corporation, as unit volume and revenues continued their rapid growth."

Or if the news is not so good: "This was a challenging quarter for us, as the events in Europe and Japan severely impacted sales, but we expect an upturn in the second quarter and continued growth during the year as we continue to increase our advertising and marketing efforts."

Whether the news is good or bad, I strongly believe in starting off with a characterizing statement.

That should be followed by the three or four headline points, such as the ones we developed in the "Preparing for the Call" section of this chapter.

It's a good idea to throw some questions into the script that you'll answer yourself, and some examples, as we will discuss in detail in Chapter 15, "Winning at the Lectern." After reporting that a new product exceeded its sales targets, you could add, "The response to the new Apex cell phone amazed even us. People were lined up for over three blocks to get into our Manhattan store two hours before opening. And why? Because this product is unlike anything on the market today."

And, finally, don't exclude significant bad news from the script. You're going to have to deal with it in the Q&A anyway, so it's best to get out in front of the issue. Outline it, explain it, and offer a remedy where possible.

One of the things many companies don't do and I think they should do is to close the call with a summary from the CEO rather than just saying "Thanks and good-bye" after the last question. Here's a sample of how such a conclusion might read:

> *So, as we said, while we did not quite hit the targets we had set for this quarter, I am still encouraged by our growth in emerging markets, as well as the successful launches of Retrofit and Neofit in Europe and Asia. We expect to see these products positively affect our P&L and cash by the end of next quarter. And, we look forward to giving you more about this at our Investor Day in New York next month.*

Earnings News Release

The news release is also a very important document in connection with an earnings call. The best releases have three or four bullet points that summarize the results between the headline and the first line of text. Here's an example:

PDQ, Inc., Revenue, Sales up for Third-Quarter

- Turnaround plan taking effect
- Revenue increased 5%
- Sales up 7%
- Earnings per share up 2.3%

NEW YORK, N.Y., October 25, 2010—PDQ, INC. (NYSE: PDQ) today reported that third-quarter 2010 total revenue rose 5% year over year (3% in local currency) to $2.6 billion. Sales were up 7%, largely due to a 20% increase in spending on advertising.

There were increases in all categories, with the largest coming from the government and non-profit sectors.

Third-quarter operating profit of $282 million was 5% (or $15 million) lower than the 2009 level, due to restructuring expenses and increased advertising costs. Peter D. Quohog, chairman and CEO, commented, "Our top-line growth shows that our turnaround plan is beginning to produce results. We're obviously pleased about this. However, as we have frequently stated, the turnaround is a lengthy process and there will be bumps in the road."

Since some publications carry only the first three or four paragraphs of such a release, it's important to get the CEO's quote in early, preferably by the third paragraph, as you see in this example.

Emerging Issues and Trends

Success in any investor communication requires being up to date on shareholder concerns and the issues that might have an impact on future earnings.

One area of increasing emphasis is social responsibility. Stephen L. Brown, senior director of corporate governance and associate general counsel at TIAA-CREF, a financial services organization and the leading provider of retirement services in the academic, research, medical, and cultural fields, says

"Social and environmental issues are very important in the corporate governance field these days. All those issues from the '70s are back now, but in greater force."

Says Brown, "Today's CEO needs to be quite conversant on social and environmental issues and speak on them. That's an issue of leadership. If you don't manage your climate change risk, you may see Congress pass a law that destroys your company; or if you don't have the safety measures in place and all of a sudden your Deepwater Horizon rig blows up, people die, you pollute the Gulf, and shareholders lose 50 to 60 percent of their value."

So the question of social responsibility needs to be on everybody's radar, on everybody's website, and at least considered for everybody's agenda as preparations are made for investor communication.

Investor Days

Investor days are good for certain types of companies but less useful for others. I think there is real value in a consumer products company scheduling one every year or two. It gives analysts a chance to sample the products and hear directly from unit heads who are not usually available on earnings calls. There are two great advantages to this. One is that more depth can be provided on something like an important new product or product line. A second is the opportunity for the company to show its bench strength through the participation of key executives—an important factor because CEO succession is always high on the list of concerns of investors.

They are also useful for a company that makes products such as medical devices. Theirs is an industry of rapid innovation in which the advantages of a new product might not be readily apparent. A new product display at the investor day gives analysts a chance to see and handle the devices and talk to company officials who can effectively explain how they advance medical care or reduce costs.

It's going to take several days to properly prepare for an investor day. Everyone who will speak must be separately rehearsed on camera with playback and critiquing to refine the delivery. Then the Q&A process should proceed along the same lines as the earnings call—identification of potential questions, selection of key points, and video-recorded rehearsal. Once that is done, the entire group should run through the program together to assure smooth transitions, avoid any materials overlap, and decide who will handle what questions.

While it's not technically the CEO's job, there is an aspect of the presentation that should not be overlooked. I have been through far too many investor day presentations where PowerPoint slides were unreadable from the back half of the room. It wouldn't hurt for the CEO to take a moment to walk back and check that out, too.

The Annual Meeting

In general, the annual meeting is not the battleground or the news event that it once was. There are a number of reasons for this. One is that disgruntled shareholders no longer have to wait for that meeting to air their dissatisfaction. There are plenty of social media outlets that offer such opportunities.

In addition, many companies have shifted their meetings to remote locations to minimize adverse media coverage, especially when they are expecting picketing or some other demonstration from a group such as a labor union. Far more TV cameras will be on the scene for such a demonstration in Manhattan, New York City, than will show up in Manhattan, Kansas. Proximity to the event definitely affects television coverage, and a protesting organization is likely to get fewer pickets to show up in Kansas.

During my broadcast news days in New York, I often surmised that you could get hordes of microphones and cameras to show up in midtown if a dozen people did a demonstration on even an insignificant issue on a slow news day. After all, the event would be in close proximity to all the big television and radio stations and, who knows, it just might turn into something interesting. It's worth sending a reporter or crew over to check it out, but it generally takes tornadoes or some other natural disaster to lure the cameras to the hinterlands. A contentious annual meeting just won't do it.

A cautionary note, however: TV and the Internet are unlikely to carry video that protesters shoot of themselves peacefully marching and chanting, but throw one protestor out of your meeting bodily, and that video is likely to go viral.

Suppose that you know in advance that a group is headed for your meeting with a strong agenda to force you to justify or change your practices. You'll need to do some good upfront work before the meeting to be sure your position on the issues is publicly and clearly stated. The company website is the obvious vehicle for this because it is a place where negatives can be addressed without calling special attention to them.

Another factor in the diminishing interest and level of drama at annual meetings is the age in which we live. There is intense daily coverage of business on television, in print, and online. Business leaders frequently face questions and complaints on key issues, so there is no need for shareholders to wait for that annual meeting to have most questions answered.

Companies have also gotten smarter about handling vociferous critics who take the microphone. Whereas you once might have seen an angry confrontation with the chairman that made the evening news, today you're more likely to hear the chairman say, "Thank you for your input, Ms. Smith. Your views will be taken into consideration." That pretty much closes off Ms. Smith's opportunity for publicity unless she can garner an on-camera interview after the meeting.

The National Investor Relations Institute (NIRI) surveys its public company members every year on their annual meeting practices.

The 2012 survey (NIRI Executive Alert, posted and emailed to members March 30, 2012) with over 200 respondents, confirmed what most of us already know: interest in these events continues to decline, and attendance is getting smaller all of the time.

Here are some of NIRI's findings:

- 67 percent of those responding report 50 or fewer annual meeting attendees.
- Primary attendees are investors, employees, and retirees.
- The annual meeting lasts one hour or less for 84 percent of those responding.
- 57 percent have an investor presentation portion, with the CEO presenting 92 percent of the time and the CFO 22 percent.
- 93 percent include a Q&A portion.
- 32 percent broadcast their annual meeting, and nearly all (93 percent) do so through webcasting.
- 3 percent hold a strictly electronic/virtual meeting; 7 percent plan to do so in the future.

While much of this is not surprising, a couple of things did jump out at me. One was that only 57 percent have an investor presentation portion of the meeting. I would have assumed it to be much higher.

Another is that 93 percent include a Q&A portion in the meeting. How do the other 7 percent get by without doing it? I would think that investors who are not allowed to raise questions during the meeting might storm the head table afterward for answers.

And then there is the question of 3 percent of the respondents holding strictly electronic/virtual meetings, with 7 percent planning to go that route soon. I expect this trend to accelerate in coming years.

The survey also showed that companies are spending less time and resources preparing for these meetings. Why not? The stakes are lower than they were, and there is no shortage of demands on the time of C-level executives.

Preparing for an annual meeting is very much like preparing for an earnings call. You need to:

- Identify the key issues and likely questions
- Rehearse and refine opening statements
- Prepare and rehearse everyone who might be confronted with a question, either during the meeting or on the way out the door

Face-to-Face Contact

Another important area of CEO communication is direct contact with large investors. A person who has invested a huge chunk of money in a company often wants instant and complete answers to new developments and may quickly pick up the phone and demand them. The CEO needs to be ready for that call at all times, with a complete set of notes on the topic in easy reach.

Face-to-face and small group meetings with big investors are also critical arenas. Here again, preparation is vital. While the investors will likely want a lot of detail, and it must be provided, the CEO still needs to focus on the three key points that really summarize the company's story. Sufficient time will also need to be spent preparing for all likely questions. The input of a good investor relations officer is critical in all of these situations, both in preparation for the event and as a fact-provider when the discussion moves into areas requiring an extensive amount of detail or numbers.

The CEO's demeanor is especially important in these settings. Here is where "presence" really comes into play. In addition to projecting a friendly, open image that says transparency, bottom-line answers and good eye contact are critical. And to go back to an important point from Chapter 3, listening is as important as talking. More than anything else, investors want to be sure the CEO is listening.

The Worst Earnings Call Ever?

As stated earlier, all investor relations are important, but the earnings call is the one most in the spotlight. We've all seen and heard some pretty good ones and some pretty bad ones. But what was the worst ever?

That dubious distinction may belong to SLM Corp, commonly known as Sallie Mae, American's largest student loan company. A bad call in December 2007, following a failed takeover deal, knocked the bottom out of investor confidence.

The CEO, new to the job, obviously had not prepared well for the call, and his handling of it hardly contributed to investor confidence. He evaded analysts' questions, insulted some of them, and refused to give details on subjects he himself had raised in his opening remarks.

Just when it appeared matters couldn't get worse, they did. Thinking the microphones were off at the end of the call, he muttered to his IRO, "Let's get the f*** out of here." Not only was it heard by everyone still listening, but the story made the mainstream media.

Needless to say, Wall Street was not impressed. A torrent of "sell" orders followed, immediately sending the stock down 20 percent to a five-year low.

Trading was 7 times the normal volume. The stock lost 50 percent of its value in the ensuing 6 months, and the company's credit rating dipped to near junk bond level.

Obviously, not all of that could be blamed on a bad earnings call, but that rough start certainly didn't help.

In sum, the investor relations challenge for CEOs is formidable. One slip could conceivably cost the corporation millions in valuation. Conversely, and more positively, good performances in this arena can add value to both the company and its top officer. Careful, thorough planning and preparation are the keys to winning with this audience.

Tips

- Thorough preparation is essential to success in all interactions with shareholders.
- Remember that shareholders and others are increasingly demanding transparency.
- Be aware that social responsibility issues have come to the fore and often influence investment decisions.
- All communication with shareholders must be based on the four Cs—Clear, concise, credible, and delivered with confidence.
- A quarterly earnings call is a statement of a company's progress, not just reporting of numbers.
- Remember: investors want to be heard. Be sure you listen as much as talk.

Notes

1. DiPiazza, Samuel A. and Robert Eccles. *Building the Public Trust: The Future of Corporate Reporting*, Hoboken, NJ: Wiley, 2002 and Eccles, Robert, Robert H. Herz, E. Mary Keegan, David M. H. Phillips. *The Value Reporting Revolution: Moving Beyond the Earnings Game*, Hoboken, NJ: Wiley, 2001.
2. Bennis, Warren, Daniel Goleman, James O'Toole, and Patricia Ward Biederman. *Transparency: Creating a Culture of Candor*, San Francisco, Jossey-Bass, 2008.

CHAPTER 9

Employees: A Vital Audience

"People just like to see you in person and like to do Q&A. I think there ultimately isn't really a substitute for just getting out and seeing people."

—Glenn Britt, Chairman and CEO, Time Warner Cable.

The leader of a Philadelphia-based corporation once famously declared that a CEO's only constituency is the shareholders. He was dead wrong.

Yes, investors buy and sell the stock, but they don't make a company successful. Success requires communication with and support from a wide variety of constituents. The list can include customers, bankers, government officials, and the news media, but it would be hard to argue that any of them are more important than employees.

One of the CEO's most important jobs is to motivate the work force. Motivated employees are more productive, likely to stay longer, and be more loyal to the organization, and reducing turnover saves companies money every single day. So does increased productivity. The way employees perceive the CEO and their role in the organization can have a lot to do with the level of success a company enjoys.

Employees want to feel some kinship with the chief executive. Employee loyalty is at or near an all-time low these days, and one reason is that the work force often feels used, expendable, underpaid, and underappreciated. In other words, "The boss is fat and comfortable, and just doesn't care about us."

This has been exacerbated by the growing disparity in compensation between those at the top of the corporate ladder and those at the bottom. It is a global problem and one that has troubled many concerned CEOs. It is not a healthy situation.

A *USA Today* article in March 2011 quoted a MetLife study that found employee loyalty at a three-year low but said employers were "precariously unaware of the morale meltdown."[1]

At the same time, the story said, the American Psychological Association reported that 4 in 10 employees said that a heavy workload, unrealistic job expectations, and long hours were causing significant worker stress. The report said morale fell and stress levels skyrocketed as cost-cutting employers froze wages, slashed bonuses, and asked workers to assume the duties of laid-off colleagues during the downturn. Insecurity is another factor—"will I be the next to go?"—and insecure employees are unlikely to be high in loyalty.

So it's not unusual for today's companies to face morale and productivity problems. While many in a company share in the responsibility to improve the situation, the CEO sets the tone and the policies for the company and thus must take the lead in bringing morale to its highest level.

Many CEOs fear that if the economy continues to improve, companies will see further problems: a drain of employees as new jobs open up, increasing costs, and disrupting operations. Taking the proper actions now to create a satisfied work force can reduce the likelihood of significant losses.

Numerous studies over the years have shown that pay level is not the primary reason for job satisfaction or dissatisfaction. That may have changed somewhat recently as many people struggle to maintain their lifestyles on less income, but the reason most consistently cited over the years as the biggest factor in job satisfaction is the chance to do meaningful work and be recognized for it.

CVS/Caremark CEO Larry Merlo agrees: "Employees want to feel like doing their job well is going to make a difference for the company and, at the end of the day, they'll be recognized and rewarded for that."

Face-to-Face Is Best

How can a CEO communicate with employees and motivate them when an organization has thousands of people spread over wide geographies?

It's great when the leader can personally meet a lot of employees, but a high volume of one-to-one communication is usually impractical, especially when the CEO rules over a far-flung empire. Glenn Britt's Time Warner Cable, for example, spans much of the United States. Further, as challenging as that is, it's even harder for a CEO to provide the personal touch in companies that have operations in many countries and on several continents.

Face-to-face communication has a terrific impact. People love to "press the flesh" with leaders. It's a rare circumstance in which a CEO, whose previous image was positive or neutral, did not find that a meeting with rank-and-file employees resulted in increased morale and loyalty.

In a visit to a large factory, for example, the CEO may have a chance to shake hands with only a few people. But if the response is favorable, word will quickly spread about "what a nice guy he is" or "he really cares about us." That sort of reaction has great value.

Smart CEOs show their faces in as many company locations as they can, especially in countries far removed from headquarters. Long-time Avon CEO Andrea Jung estimates that she spoke to more than 100,000 sales representatives in 2011 alone, "from Johannesburg to Delhi," with stops in China, Brazil, and many other places in between.

But, realistically, most heads of large companies can meet face-to-face or speak in meetings to only a small percentage of the work force. So they communicate with employees in other ways: through such modern communication tools as videos, website posts, and emails. In fact, video has become so pervasive in internal communication that many CEOs have found they have to improve their on-camera technique. That's something not generally taught in MBA programs, and it doesn't come naturally.

The Personal Touch

Town halls and employee meetings are valuable tools in motivating employees. But in focusing on the medium, people too often overlook the message. The message must always be tailored to the audience.

I once was preparing a U.S.-based CEO for a meeting with employees in Singapore. His talk, well prepared by his communications department, began with a "thank you" to the Singapore team for all it had done to contribute to the company's success. Good start, but wait a minute. I asked the CEO, "What exactly have they done?" He replied, "I'm not sure, but it's a strong operation for us." I replied, "We have to find out and mention specifics. Otherwise, it will sound like the same old boilerplate, and nobody will be convinced that you put any real value on the Singapore operation."

We found it, and the talk was a huge success.

If you want to make someone happy and satisfied, praise that person for something that he or she regards with special pride. As I said before, numerous surveys have shown that employee loyalty is more closely tied to job satisfaction and recognition than salary. Insincere blanket praise can be worse than saying nothing at all.

Heading a small organization or a small headquarters of a larger company offers its own challenges. You are on view and, in effect, on trial every day.

I worked at an all-news radio station in New York City in the 1970s, and I will never forget the debut of one of our less popular news directors.

He gave an opening pep talk to the staff, standing in front of the door to his office. He told us (falsely, it turned out) how he would welcome our input on matters of importance to the news operation. He said, "My door will always be open."

And with that, without taking any questions, he turned, went into his office, and closed the door.

It was rarely open again during his tenure. He was often the talk of the newsroom, and not in a way any manager would desire.

Using Today's Resources

A CEO needs to be a familiar face and voice to a company's employees. In my view, most companies don't use him or her enough. A video in which the CEO speaks to workers, say, once a month, can be very valuable. It can make them feel in the loop and appreciated.

If I were producing such a video, I would have it run no more than three to five minutes. It would include the following: an overview of the latest developments in the company, the singling out of a particular group or individual for praise for a particular job well done, and a summary of some of the company's plans going forward.

I'd also institute a monthly CEO's award for excellence and have it presented to the individual by the CEO—captured for the video feed, of course.

Performance awards are a strong motivator, especially when they are tied to corporate goals. I once worked for a mid-sized public relations firm that prided itself on the quality of its writing. The agency offered prizes for the best writing of the month and the year. The CEO would hand them out personally with a bit of fanfare.

At one point, I won a monthly award for the writing in a proposal I had submitted to a large bank. My unit didn't even win the business, but the award was about writing, not sales. The prize was a handsome down jacket that I wore for years. Every time someone commented on it, I recounted the story about how I had won it and how the agency valued good writing. It was a terrific morale booster.

Regular bylined articles in a company publication, *A Letter from the CEO*, also can build loyalty. So can setting up an email system where the employees can make suggestions or ask questions of the CEO that the chief executive, or someone designated by him or her, will provide a brief, direct, and honest answer for, always with a note that Mr./Ms. _____ appreciates and thanks you for your input and your loyalty to the company.

Some of the best of these exchanges can then be put in company publications and on the company's website.

What I am suggesting here will not take a huge amount of the leader's time. But these steps can play a significant role in communicating the company's values and its appreciation of its workers.

Two Good Small-Scale Examples

Two of the best executives I've ever seen, in terms of building staff loyalty, worked for small organizations at the time. Bob Pearson, who was then head of the public relations firm GCI, once told his staff, "You don't work for me; I work for you. You are my client. My job is to help make you as successful as possible." The staff loved him.

Steve Caldeira, when he headed a unit of the National Restaurant Association, invited me to a small dinner he was holding for his public relations staff. At such a dinner, some executives would simply raise a toast to the team, say they were great, and move on to the food. But not Caldeira. He went around the room, calling out each of the dozen or so people by name and praising them for some specific thing they had accomplished and were personally proud of. Needless to say, he had a loyal and dedicated staff.

Caldeira, now head of the International Franchise Association, says the key to successful employee communication is to be "upfront, direct, and respectful. Always give them a heads-up on what you're going to communicate, and seek input. Remember, communication is a two-way street."

What management does is as important as—or more so than—what management says. I once worked with a CEO of a large utility company in New England. When it came time to break for lunch, he told me, "Our senior management always takes its lunch in the company cafeteria. It sends a good message to our employees."

So I went through the line with him and the other managers and got my lunch. I located an empty table and started heading toward it, but the CEO stopped me. "Not here," he said, pointing to a separate dining area up a flight of stairs. "The management eats up there."

So we took our trays up the stairs to that higher dining area, the one that looked down on the cafeteria and was reserved for management only.

The implication was clear: management is "above" you, looking down. From the standpoint of employee morale, they would have been better off to order in.

By contrast, UPS has long had a policy of its executive team eating in the company cafeteria and sitting at the common tables. In addition, executives are not permitted to eat at their desks. Former UPS CEO Jim Kelly put it to me this way: "Our offices are our workplace. For a driver, the truck is the workplace. We don't allow our drivers to eat in their trucks, so we don't eat in our offices."

That sends a strong message of fairness. So did an experience with a later UPS CEO, Mike Eskew, who offered to drive me to the train station after a day of rehearsal for a major presentation. When we walked to his car in the company garage, it was not parked in a special reserved slot next to the door, as I expected, but some distance away in the common parking area. That, too, spoke volumes.

Henry Ford, the founder of the Ford Motor Company, is said to have had an employee motivation technique that was particularly effective. He would outline an idea and, instead of saying, "I want this done," would say, "I wonder if we can do it."

It's hard to imagine anyone saying no.

Employees are your ambassadors to the world. They are your most important company resource, and they are a very, very expensive component to replace. That makes them one of your most important audiences. Take the time and care to communicate often and effectively with them.

Tips

- Put a high priority on employee communication.
- Be upfront, direct, and respectful.
- Praise employees in specific, not general, terms.
- Create a climate that encourages their input.
- Use all of the tools of modern technology to stay connected with the work force.
- Avoid actions that appear to separate you from your employees.

Note

1. Laura Petrecca, "Employee loyalty is at a three-year low," *USA Today*, March 28, 2011.

CHAPTER 10

CEOs and Boards: Times Have Changed

"Perhaps nothing is more vital in your role as a CEO than how you present to, and communicate with, your board."
—*Tom Wajnert and Stephen A. Miles, executive consultants*

Boards of directors are not what they used to be. As a result, many CEOs are finding they've had to change some of the ways they deal with those in the boardroom. Today's boards are generally more active and more demanding of the CEO.

Not too long ago, sitting on a board of directors in many companies could be a pretty good deal. You could go to four meetings a year, collect a nice stipend for it, and just basically listen to the CEO spin tales about how well he was running the company.

Times have changed. Boards are increasingly coming under criticism for sitting idly by while a "cowboy" CEO makes big mistakes. There are new federal laws that put increased pressure and responsibility on boards. Business media commentators and stock analysts don't hesitate to loudly chastise boards that they think should fire an underperforming CEO.

Further, big investors are putting ever-increasing pressure on CEOs to pick board members who will exercise independent judgment. Good governance groups are also pressing for more separation of the jobs of chairman and CEO.

Successful Partnership

What are the keys to a successful board-CEO relationship? In my view, two considerations override all others: the quality of the board and the CEO's ability to communicate and interact with it. The CEO who merely tells the board what he is going to do and doesn't lead a dialog about planned moves is making a very serious mistake.

Investors need to have confidence that while the board is in a partnership with the CEO, it is independent and providing valuable input in the running of the company. TIAA-CREF's Stephen Brown says investors are turned off by the "Imperial CEO." He cited one case where a CEO had three conversations with his organization's investment group in the last 12 months. Says Brown, "He had his executive team with him, but never a board member. He kept saying, 'I will tell my board, and what I have told the board is this,' etc., etc. We walked away feeling that no one in the board room was controlling anything."

The feeling that a CEO is telling the board what to do is not a comforting one for investors. It is heightened, of course, when the chief executive also holds the position of chairman and has handpicked the board.

The ideal board of directors is experienced, intelligent, engaged, and independent. Any board member who does not meet all of these qualifications should be shown the door.

Some CEOs will prepare very hard for a shareholder meeting and less so for a board meeting. This may especially be true when the corporate head has known many of the members for some time, but that can be a serious mistake.

Rule number one in dealing with any board is transparency. Never let the board get surprised or blindsided. A difficult situation or growing problem should be brought to their attention before it becomes public. It's true: "Forewarned is forearmed."

Another rule is to discuss any major plan or change of policy with them in the development stages, not once it has been put into place. A common complaint from board members is that a CEO walks in with a predetermined plan and just looks for a rubber stamp from them. That's a good way to get rejected or, at the very least, resented.

Meeting the Board Face-to-Face

How should a CEO prepare for a board meeting? Basically by following the same principles and guidelines that I will outline in Chapter 15, "Winning at the Lectern," remembering that both too much and too little detail can doom a presentation.

The first meeting a new CEO has with the board is often the most important one. Impressions are formed about the CEO's personality, character, management style, and, perhaps most of all, competence. Negative impressions in that meeting will be hard to dislodge later on. First impressions have long staying power.

Volvo's CEO Persson, who ascended to the top position in late 2011, uses this preparation method before he meets his board. "I try to put myself in the shoes of the board of directors. If I were a board member having read through the material, what would I like to hear in order to come to a conclusion? If you do that, you come to the conclusion that some of the presentation that you thought was brilliant might not be so brilliant if you put yourself in the shoes of the listener."

As is true with other important presentations, an on-camera rehearsal, carefully reviewed and critiqued by a knowledgeable associate and/or consultant, is always a good idea. So is touching base on the phone with some key members to find out what is on their minds and what they think other board members will especially want to know.

Here are some of the things a CEO needs to remember in any meeting with company directors:

- First, don't assume that they recall what you told them last time or that they have followed the company's activities on a day-to-day basis. Remember: they have other jobs and interests, and they get briefed four times a year, not daily.
- It's often a good idea to start out with a brief recap of where the company stands in regard to its game plan and what might have changed since the last meeting, especially when the current situation has a lot of moving parts.
- Leaders also need to keep in mind that most board members are not likely to be financial experts. Don't expect them to ferret out the key numbers in a complex chart. Keep the presentation simple and hold the numbers-heavy charts as backup for those who want to dig deeper.
- Think visual. Use examples and illustrations to make your points memorable.
- Ask plenty of questions and seek open dialogue. After all, these are experts whose experience may be far broader than your own.
- Perhaps most important, make sure everyone is in agreement before making a major policy decision.

Relationships and Persuasion

Unless it's a birthday party or a big raise in pay, most people don't like surprises. This is true in spades with boards of directors.

One of the biggest mistakes a CEO can make is to surprise a board with a decision they won't like and on which they have had little or no input. I've heard of CEOs doing this when they felt they were on the right track and the board was not likely to go along with their plan. That is a risky strategy.

In this case, I think a wise first step is to have phone or face-to-face conversations with board members in which the CEO lays out the rationale for change or a new direction, then asks for input on possible solutions. This is a meeting in which the chief executive should follow the formula laid out in Chapter 3, "Active Listening": 20 percent talking and 80 percent listening.

Regular phone conversations with board members are a good idea anyway. It reminds them that they and their views are valued (if not always followed) and shows that you are a leader who listens.

Once the subject has been discussed individually with board members, the CEO will have a better sense of what the likely reaction will be and can also be ready with responses to objections and tough questions.

The next step comes at the board meeting. I think it's a good idea to start by outlining the problem, or opportunity, that is the impetus for the planned move. Then I would summarize the comments and perspectives the various board members have offered, giving all of them credit for constructive input.

At this point, I would submit the plan, outlining reasons for it and why you have decided to go this direction rather than pursuing the alternatives that have been suggested. A PowerPoint presentation can be helpful in laying out the key facts and figures.

The questions and discussions that follow will either get support for your action or send you back to the drawing board. Either way, the board has done its job, and you have built loyalty that will serve you well in the future.

What Your Board Gives You

Some CEOs seem to regard a board of directors as a necessary nuisance, but the smart ones regard it as an essential contributor to the company's success.

Jim Kilts, who gave the board abundant credit for the success he had at Gillette, shared his formula: "I like nail chewers on my board because they're going to keep you honest: people with high integrity, high business acumen, and who are very objective. We had a terrific board."

Big investors have more faith in a company whose board is known for its independence.

TIAA-CREF's Brown told me, "Having a board that has the ability to express independent thought is so important. It's so much more than simply having intelligence. The Enron board was well-heeled with high credentials, but what were they thinking when they were asked to waive their code of conduct?"

That decision was a critical factor in Enron's demise.

At no time is a board's support of its CEO more important than when the company leader is contemplating a move that shareholders might not like. Covidien's Almeida tells this story: "We bought a company in 2010 for $2.6 billion. I was convinced that it was the right thing for Covidien in the long term. Convinced! I knew the markets, I knew the growth, I knew the economics behind that deal. But when we announced it, we had a very negative reaction from the investors."

But the board fully backed the move, and Almeida was able to hold his ground against unhappy shareholders. "We did the right thing," he says. "That was a great acquisition. You've got to be able to have the board support so you can take criticism like that."

He concluded, "Today, we're all heroes."

Tips

- Pick a board that is intelligent, engaged, and independent.
- Be transparent. Never let the board get blindsided.
- Don't assume too much knowledge.
- Present your briefings in clear, plain language, with illustrations and examples.
- Consult with the board before finalizing major decisions, not after.
- Ask plenty of questions and seek dialogue.

PART III

The Media Factor

CHAPTER 11

The News Media: Opportunity and Peril

"Nothing a CEO does, not one thing, has as much potential for victory or disaster as a media interview."

—Ken Scudder

Facing the media is one of the most important and often least desired duties of a CEO.

True, the price of failure can be high, but when intelligently managed, media interviews can pay off big for a company. Many will move stock, and if the executive is properly prepared and executes the game plan, the likelihood of a damaging failure will be very low.

Here is a simple fact: both journalists and the general public put more trust in people whose voices and faces they know than in strangers. That factor alone demonstrates why CEOs need to have a media role.

Media interviews are especially important when a CEO is new to the job. First impressions last a long time, and a negative one can be hard to reverse. The initial impression must be that the CEO has talent, intelligence, a good working knowledge of the company, and a plan for future success. Perhaps just as important, the person needs to be seen as friendly and open.

That is an image that all CEOs need to have all the time.

The key to success is picking the right venues and topics, and then thoroughly preparing for the encounter.

More Places and Opportunities to Appear

While some people see interviews as challenges or threats, most interviews actually represent opportunity.

Business television shows proliferate around the globe these days. Overall, they tend to be very positive in their approach to business. They have strong viewership among investors, but it is not just investors who want to the see the positive public face of a business leader. The CEO represents the company's employees. They want to see the boss project the organization's image in a positive light, and people who deal with the company in a major way, such as customers or vendors, also wish to see a strong positive image projected by the leader.

A CEO client of mine, the head of an Internet brokerage firm, made his first major TV appearance on CNBC a few years ago. Though nervous, he handled it well and was praised by the program's anchors for his performance.

He was pleased (and relieved), but the good news did not end there. As we rode back from Fort Lee, New Jersey, to his office in New York City, his BlackBerry lit up with emails from staff members in various parts of the world. Especially noteworthy were two from Sydney and Singapore, key markets for his company. They carried messages like "Great work, chief. You've made our job easier," and "This interview is going to help us in the marketplace."

The interview subsequently served as a good introduction piece to show to both investors and clients. It effectively outlined the company's mission, offerings, and financial prospects in a clear and convincing way. That one interview was worth untold thousands of dollars in benefits to the company.

Business publications and business sections of newspapers have also expanded greatly. They represent a significant opportunity for a company to tell its story in a favorable setting. Passing up potentially positive interviews is leaving opportunity, and therefore money, on the table.

Being a known and respected leader has particular advantages when trouble strikes. No one exemplified this principle better than Lee Iacocca did during the fall and subsequent government rescue of Chrysler in the 1980s. When Iacocca told members of Congress and the public that he could restore Chrysler to health, they believed him, and he did it. BP and Toyota would have had more credibility when their crises hit if their leaders had been familiar, respected figures to the American public (see Chapter 21, "Crisis: A CEO's Supreme Test").

You Have to Appear

I have often heard from company leaders "I don't want to be in the public eye. I'm not the story; the company is."

"That's right," I respond, "but you are the face of the company. No one else can fill that role."

CEO speechwriter and consultant Jeff Shesol puts it this way: "CEOs have to drive the company's message, to assert thought leadership where that can be reasonably asserted and to help lead a conversation, one that helps a company achieve its goals, whatever they are."

The right interviews in the right media are vital to meeting this responsibility.

A CEO must be a limited edition. Overexposure can be as big a problem as underexposure. A CEO who handles media exposure as an ego trip can do more harm than good.

What are the warning signs for someone who coaches a CEO that the leader is getting star-struck to the detriment of the business?

Steve Soltis, director of executive communications for Coca-Cola, puts it this way: "Does the CEO still speak in the collective 'we,' or is she or he slipping into the 'I' syndrome? If it's the latter, you've got a problem. Also, look at the person's schedule. Are public appearances driving the calendar more than other key aspects of the job? If so, you might have a problem."

How should a PR professional decide whether to accept or reject an interview offer for the CEO? Covidien's Kraus says he starts this way: "benefit to the company, subject matter, and whether it's broadcast or print."

A few other considerations could be added here: size and demographic of audience, attitude of interviewer(s), and timeliness.

There is great benefit to putting a CEO in front of the media after a company has a strong quarter. But it's also a good idea (sometimes) to go public in the face of bad news. The CEO can put the situation in perspective and give reassurance that the company is on top of the problem and able to successfully handle it.

A good example comes from JetBlue Airlines. The morning after an in-air incident when a pilot apparently had a psychotic episode and had to be subdued by the passengers and crew, CEO David Barger went on *Today* and faced the music. Some companies would merely have said, "The incident is under investigation," and left it at that.

He praised the cabin crew and the passengers for their actions, saying it was because of training that the incident was resolved without anyone being harmed. The questioning was tough, and the answers were mostly, but not always, convincing. For example, he kept referring to the incident as a medical situation, which obviously downplayed the seriousness of it. He should have referred to it as "the captain behaving irrationally."

But the point was clear. The CEO stepped up. In the military, battle stars are won in combat. In business, they are often won in the successful handling of bad news.

If there is any question of danger to the public's health and safety, the CEO must be front and center, and the news media represent the best tool for that job.

In good news or bad, there is nothing as powerful as the CEO speaking out in the media. It is a requirement for today's business leaders and is a great chance for them to showcase their leadership and qualifications. The next two chapters will show you how to properly prepare yourself for this most important venue.

Tips

- Consider media appearances to be an essential part of a CEO's job.
- Take advantage of the opportunities offered through business media outlets.
- Pick the appropriate media forums to deliver the right message to the right audience.
- Accept interviews that will align with the company's policies and objectives.
- Be ready to step forward publicly in the face of bad news.

CHAPTER 12

Winning in the Media

"It is always a risk to speak to the press; they are likely to report what you say."

—Hubert H. Humphrey, former U.S. vice president

It is impossible to count the number of times I've heard executives say, "I never deal with the media. It's a battle you can't win."

The fact is businesses leaders win with the media most of the time, and almost invariably when they lose the damage has been self-inflicted.

High-level business executives, especially CEOs, have a huge advantage in the world of media. Because of their prestigious positions, they are generally treated with deference. After all, a CEO interview is a nice "catch" for a journalist, and rude treatment could close the door on future interviews. That doesn't mean the leader can expect only "softball" questions. Far from it. But it does mean that the tone will generally be respectful (in some cases practically worshipful), and the questions are not likely to stray far from those topics that were agreed upon when the interview was scheduled.

Should the conversation stray, the well-prepared executive is ready to cope with it.

How to Judge a Media "Winner"

When I began my media training career, I wasn't sure that I knew how to teach people to be good at being interviewed. After all, I'd spent my time on the other side of the microphone. I had seldom been interviewed. I was the person firing the questions, not the one who had to field them.

How would I teach executives how to come out as winners in media interviews?

My boss at Carl Byoir & Associates, Carolyn Walden, showed me the way. She asked me to name half a dozen business and government leaders in New York who were very good at dealing with the media and thus got a lot of favorable coverage. I gave her some names of people I had interviewed, and she agreed with them.

Then she asked me to name some who did not do well in media interviews. I gave her another list, and again she agreed. Then she said, "So, you have two groups here; one that you liked to interview as a broadcaster, and another that you did not. One that got a lot of good media coverage, and one that did not. What did they do differently?"

I thought for a moment, and then said, "Here it is. The winners come in with a story to tell, and they know how to tell it. They take positive control of the interview, satisfying the questions and going on to tell you interesting things you did not know or did not think to ask about. The losers just answer questions. You generally don't get a very good interview from them."

She agreed. I have based my executive training on that premise for the last three decades.

Your Purpose in an Interview

When it comes to being interviewed, I tell every client to "Think Opportunity." Every interview is an opportunity to improve your and your company's image and standing with the public. My thinking is that you should welcome the chance to be interviewed, even in the toughest circumstances, because it gives you the chance to tell your story, handle any criticisms that may be out there, and show the quality of your leadership and your organization.

The heart of this philosophy is never do an interview for the purpose of answering questions. Never!

Do every interview to tell your story.

Don't you have to answer the questions? Yes, you do, but that is not your purpose any more than your purpose when you got up this morning was to put on your shoes. You had to put on your shoes to do what you wanted, but that was not your purpose in waking.

You judge the success of every interview by this standard:

1. Did I get my points across?
2. Did I foresee and successfully handle the negatives?
3. Did I have credibility?

These are the only criteria that you should use. It doesn't matter if the interviewer liked you (although it certainly helps), and it doesn't even matter if you think you convinced the interviewer of your point of view. Your job is not to win over the interviewer; your job is to make your points, handle the negatives, and be credible.

Do not rely on the interviewer to lead you to your key points. It's your job to see that they get into the interview.

Your interview mind-set must be this: you are a newsmaker, not a criminal defendant.

Think of yourself as a teacher and the interviewer as a student. A teacher comes into class with a lesson plan, a body of information to be communicated to the students. He or she doesn't stand in front of the room and say, "Okay, what do you want to know about Shakespeare?"

If a student asks a question that is off the teacher's agenda, say a chemistry question in a physics class, what will the teacher do? Engage in a long discussion of the basics of chemistry? No. She will briefly answer the question, and then go back to talking about physics. That is exactly what you should do in dealing with the news media.

Keep this in mind: while journalists expect their questions to be answered, they don't always know what questions to ask. You do them a favor if you fill in relevant information that they neglected or did not know to seek. Remember, you are the expert on your subject, not they.

One of the most frustrating moments for a broadcaster is one that I experienced too many times to count. You have just conducted an interview—it's over, having either been broadcast live or been recorded for later use. You walk the guest to the door and thank him for his participation. Then, as you are saying good-bye, he tells you something about the story that is more interesting than anything he said on the air! Like, for example, mentioning an innovative new product the company is developing.

The dialogue that follows is always the same:

VS: Why didn't you tell me that on the air?
Guest: Because you didn't ask me about it.
VS: That's because I wasn't aware of it.
Guest: Oh, I just thought you weren't interested.

This exchange represents a loss for both journalist and newsmaker, as well as the audience. The best part of the story has not been told.

Taking Control of the Interview

The message is clear: the executive needs to immediately take positive control of an interview if the questions are not the ones that relate to his points.

Simply answering a reporter's questions without volunteering any additional information can lead to a dull interview at best and a bad one at worst. Most of all, doing so is a lost opportunity.

In every interview you should come in with three key points. I call these points "Must Airs." As mentioned before, your purpose in this interview is to "sell" these Must Air points.

Must Airs are short, declarative, provable sentences that, taken together, add up to the message you want to convey in the interview. I'll explore the nature of Must Airs later in this chapter.

It's easy to make your Must Air points if the reporter asks directly about them, but how do you get to your story if the questions don't lead you there? The technique I teach is called "satisfy and steer." It involves *satisfying* a non-agenda question as briefly as you can and then *steering* to a point you came to discuss.

Here's how it looks on a chart.

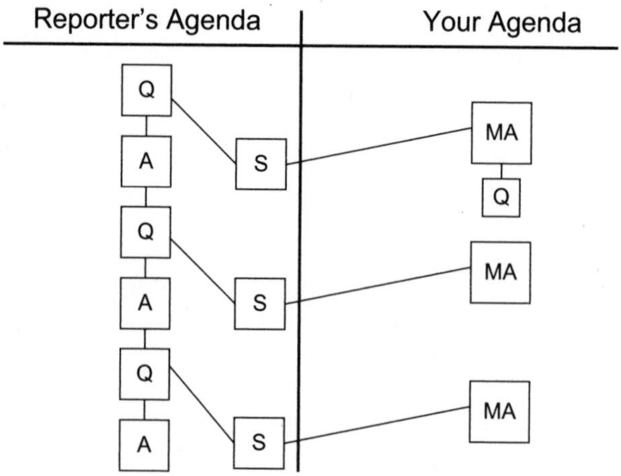

Satisfy and Steer Chart

A reporter comes into an interview with an agenda. That agenda is to get a story, and the reporter's method for getting that story is by asking questions. This is represented on the left side of the chart.

You also come into the interview with an agenda—to tell your story. Your method for telling your story is by getting your Must Airs into the reporter's story. This is represented on the right side of the chart.

In a typical interview, with an interviewee who has not been media trained, a reporter asks a question that is not exactly on the subject's agenda. Being well schooled by parents, society, teachers, and so on to be straightforward, the interviewee gives a direct answer to that question. However, this answer does not contain a Must Air.

The reporter comes with the next question, which 99 percent of the time will draw from the answer the interviewee just gave. Why? That's how conversations work. The next time you see two people talking, either an interview on TV or just a face-to-face conversation, note how many times what Person B says or asks comes directly out of the last thing Person A just said.

So, without satisfying and steering, we're onto the second question of the interview, and our subject still hasn't made a Must Air point. Because this question also isn't directly related to a Must Air, and the answer isn't either, the conversation goes for a few minutes without our interviewee making a single point. Based on our criteria for judging an interview, this cannot be considered a success.

Instead, what should happen, as the chart shows, is that when the reporter asks that first question, the interviewee should satisfy the question and then proceed to one or more of his Must Air points.

What does "satisfy the question" mean? It means giving a brief answer that gets to the heart of the question but doesn't go into a ton of detail before steering. Satisfying can be as short as "yes," "no," or "I don't know," or it can be a two-sentence answer. The important thing is that it is briefer than the points to which the interviewee steers.

But won't the interviewer object to your going off in a somewhat different direction? Not if the new point is interesting and relevant and adds value to the interview. Relevant to what? To the question? Not necessarily. Relevant to the topic you agreed to discuss.

Here's an example:

Question: "Is your company planning any acquisitions in the energy area?"

Answer: "No, but let me tell you what we are planning. We have three exciting new product lines ready for launch."

The newsmaker satisfied the question in one word. Now he or she is entitled to move across the page and tell the story he came to tell. Both parties win.

In this example, the next question is likely to be a request for more information on the new products. The newsmaker is now firmly in control of the process.

How can you tell when you have not successfully satisfied a question? Simple: the interviewer will ask it again. The next time you watch an interview, note when you think the subject didn't successfully satisfy the question. I'll bet you that the interviewer comes right back with it after the answer. Very often, that question starts with "Yes, but I asked you. . . ."

That's an embarrassing situation for the newsmaker, as his or her lack of forthrightness has been called to everyone's attention.

I teach that at all times in an interview you are either on "your side of the page" or you need to get there right now.

Believe it or not, this process is sometimes easier to do in a hostile interview than in a friendly one. When being hit with a barrage of tough questions, the interviewee who has been well trained is primed and ready to satisfy them and get to the safety of his side of the page. However, when the questions are softer but still not directly related to the Must Airs, there can be a tendency to just answer them. After all, you're not doing any damage to yourself.

True, but you are also not taking full advantage of your opportunity, and that is a waste.

Satisfying and Steering is not something done once in an interview. It is a continual process. You should try to get your Must Airs into every interview a few times, but instead of just parroting what you said before, you should add information and go deeper into your subject.

A good entry line can be "let me tell you more about this new technology that I mentioned a moment ago."

A Common Trap

One of the biggest mistakes executives make in dealing with the media is that they sometimes get too comfortable and say things they would normally only say to close colleagues or friends. The penalty for such "loose lips" behavior can be severe.

A good example of this occurred in April 2012 when the CEO of a large Silicon Valley technology company was talking with *The Wall Street Journal*'s Alan Murray on the Journal's *Viewpoints West Forum*. It's a very casual setting and, while a video of the discussion is recorded and put online, it feels almost like a living room conversation between friends.

In a discussion about what it takes to compete globally, Murray, a friendly and informal interviewer who makes his guests feel very comfortable, asked the CEO a question about what competitor worries him the most. The chief executive named a Chinese company, then stuck his foot firmly down his throat when asked why. He complained that "They don't always play by the rules" in matters such as intellectual property protection and computer security.

Not surprisingly, Murray followed up by asking, "When you say they don't play by the rules, could you give a couple of examples?" Now sensing the deep water he was in, the CEO stumbled, fumbled, made a feeble attempt at humor and had to stop and think for several seconds to come up with an answer. When he did, it was a bad one.

It was several minutes before the executive could extricate himself from the self-inflicted trap and get on to other subjects.

An unthinking answer to a simple question turned into a widely reported gaffe.

The CEO of an unrelated company, who is not yet convinced that media encounters can be consistently won if handled right, sent me the link to the video and said, "See, that shows the danger of doing media interviews."

I replied to him, "No, that shows the danger of treating a media interview as a casual chat instead of a serious discussion that the newsmaker needs to control. The CEO should have given a brief response to the question without bringing up ethical issues and moved on to what he came to talk about. This was an embarrassment that should never have happened."

Framing the Issues

In any interview, but especially one that is at all challenging or adversarial, it's important not to let the reporter frame the issue. While you are obligated to address the questions raised, you are not obligated to use the other person's words.

Journalists don't always have time to prepare for an interview as thoroughly as you or they would like, so they sometimes ask strange questions, especially when they're not sure where to go next. Newsmakers sometimes get thrown by some of these "out of the blue" queries and fumble and stumble around a bit before regaining their composure.

This is not too likely to happen if you've framed the issues and carried the conversational ball, but it does happen from time to time. I've put together a list of some of the more common ones to help you avoid some familiar traps. I call the list "What to Say When."

Q: What keeps you awake at night?
A: Nothing in particular, but during the day my focus is on . . .

Q: What would you say is your biggest problem?
A: Our biggest challenge is . . . (plug in point).

Q: Who is your main competitor?
A: We have a number of competitors, and here's why I feel we are well positioned to continue to succeed against them.

Q: How do you personally feel about this issue?
A: I'm not here to speak for myself today but for the company. And the company's position is . . .

Q: Why won't you break down your sales by region?
A: That information is proprietary for competitive reasons, but here's what I can tell you.

Q: Do people or profits matter most?
A: Both are important to us and our shareholders. We are proud of being both profitable and known as a good place to work.

Q: Did your company act out of greed or incompetence?
A: Neither. An honest mistake was made and it has now been rectified.

Q: What would you do if . . .
A: That's a hypothetical question. Let me give you a real-world situation.

Q: We have heard a report that . . .
A: I haven't seen that report and thus can't comment on it, but let me give you the facts as I know them.

Most of all, it's important not to repeat a negative, especially in a print story. Look at these two examples.

Example 1.
Reporter: *Your company has a poor safety record.*
Executive: *No, we don't have a poor safety record.*

Example 2.
Reporter: *Your company has a poor safety record.*
Executive: *That's not true. Our safety record is good and getting better.*

In example 1, the resulting headline is likely to be "Safety Record Not Poor, Says Exec." In example 2, it's more likely to be "Safety Record Good, Says Exec."
There's a big difference.

Preparing Your Messages

Interviews tend to be mostly linear. They will often go down one line for several questions before moving another direction, so it's important that the newsmaker get to his side of the page quickly and keep coming back when off-agenda questions are asked.

The agenda should generally consist of a theme line, often in the form of a sound bite, and three Must Airs that the newsmaker will stress. Those Must Air points will need to be backed up with examples or proofs.

Here's an example:

Theme line

This company is moving in the right direction.

Must Airs

1. We have added six exciting new products in the past year.
2. We have cut costs across the board.
3. Our market share is up 3 percent this quarter alone.

I've heard of some media coaches who say to clients, "Don't worry about answering the questions; just ignore any questions you don't like and say what you want. Just lay out your key points."

I could not disagree more with this theory. Not satisfying the question destroys your credibility. This kind of behavior on television is one of the reasons so many politicians have so little credibility.

Here's how a hypothetical politician's interview might go. Let's say that the congressman agreed to go on the air to discuss the state of the economy, but the first question goes quite a different direction.

Q: Congressman, you've been accused of harassing women staff members on several occasions, and some say they may bring charges against you. How do you respond to that?

A: Fred, I've been in Congress for 20 years, and I'm proud of my record. My name is on some important legislation, and the folks back home in South Dakota know I represent them well.

Q: But what about those harassment charges?

A: We need to focus on what's important, Fred. The economy is a mess, and I have ideas for some new approaches to it. Let me give you one.

Some people might think the congressman won this round because he evaded answering the tough questions. I disagree. This kind of evasion is quickly spotted by most people, and they think less of the speaker as a result.

Keep in mind that the success of an interview is gauged by what people take away, and that includes perception as well as fact. In this case, the takeaway is that he's guilty as charged because he refused to deal with the question.

What he should have done is this:

Q: Congressman, you have been accused of harassing women staff members on several occasions, and some say they may bring suit against you. How do you respond to that?

A: Fred, I did not knowingly harass anybody, and I will fight any legal action that may result. I am meeting with each of my staff members to discuss this issue and identify what I might have said that gave that impression. I apologize to anyone I might have offended.

However, I can't let this distract me from doing my job in Congress. The economy remains a mess, and I will be presenting some new ideas to deal with it.

By addressing the question directly and satisfying it, the official has earned the right to tell his story.

General Motors Example

Every interview represents opportunity gained or lost.

A vivid example came in April 2009 after the U.S. government had bailed out and then taken effective control of General Motors.

Fritz Henderson, the newly named CEO of GM, and his team had submitted a reorganization plan to the White House panel that was responsible for overseeing the company's turnaround program. The plan was flatly rejected. Shortly thereafter, the executive appeared on *Meet the Press* with David Gregory to discuss the situation. The interview was awful, and it left viewers with even less confidence that this executive could set the company right.

Here is a transcript of the most relevant parts, with my comments on where Henderson went wrong and how he could have better handled the questions.

David Gregory: *The administration's Auto Task Force tasked General Motors with the idea of coming up with a viability plan. The company did that, and the White House rejected it flatly. There were some stinging rebukes embedded in that report. Here's just a sampling: "General Motors' plan is not viable as it is currently structured. The assumptions in GM's business plan are too* *optimistic. Progress has been far too slow." Pretty harsh reaction from the Obama White House. How did the company get it wrong?*

Fritz Henderson: *Well, as we look at the situation—first, we're very appreciative of the support, David, of the White House and the Automotive Task Force. They got up to speed very fast, in a very short period of time. They basically took a very hard look at both the assumptions, as well as the actions, in our plan. They talked about the progress that has been made. But the conclusion was "not far enough, not fast enough," and candidly that's where our charge is going forward.*

(The question was not answered: how did the company get it wrong? He should have been ready to respond briefly to this question and then move to what the company is doing now to get it right.)

Gregory: *Alright, but you were there as this report was put together, you've been there for 25 years, where do you think the company misjudged its own reality and the way forward?*

Henderson: *David, I have been with the company 25 years. Through my career I've made a lot of mistakes, as we all do. But, my job is to learn from them and look forward to make sure we get the job done.*

(Again, this is an unresponsive answer. What is the way forward? He should be giving some specifics.)

Gregory: *Your predecessor, Rick Waggoner, was pushed out by the White House, that of course is well known. Under his tenure, GM has lost $82 billion in just the last four years. The value of the stock has plunged 95 percent—it was $42 a share a year-and-a-half ago; it's $2.10 as it closed on Friday. Do you think the firing of Rick Waggoner was the right decision?*

Henderson: *David, Rick was my friend . . . is my friend, mentor; I worked for him the better part of my career. But with Rick it was always about the company, not about him. He was asked to step aside, and he did, and we need to look forward.*

(Another non-responsive answer. He should have said, "That (the decision) is not for me to decide. My job is to move the company forward, and let me tell you about some of the ways we plan to do that.")

Gregory: *Well, but part of looking forward is trying to take account for what's gone on up till now and mistakes that have been made, decisions that have been made, that the White House says were not reflective of the idea of really taking account for mistakes that have been made. Can you point to some areas where you think the company has really faltered?*

Henderson: *Well, it has been a difficult . . . you mentioned it, it has been a certainly challenging last several years. We've had challenges in a number of places around the globe, whether it's here in our home market in the United States or in Europe, and in many ways we're not the only ones that have had those problems. But, I really don't focus on that. We just need to take the mistakes that we've made, learn from 'em, not get overly invested in them, and go forward and learn from them.*

(Again, no direct response but a bundle of fluff and a vague promise.)

Gregory: *You would agree that General Motors needs to be reinvented and badly needs change.*

Henderson: *I would agree, yes.*

(He should have gone on to list some of the changes he has made or is making and what is likely to be forthcoming in the future.)

Gregory: *Now, you've been at the company for 25 years. You are an insider. Critics of the industry, and of General Motors in particular, say the culture at GM is simply too inbred. How can an insider like yourself be relied upon to make transformational change?*

Henderson: *Well, I do come to the job with 25 years of experience in the company. And having run our businesses just about everywhere around the globe, I've seen a lot of things happen in the automotive industry. I've seen good times, I've seen bad times, and we've adjusted. I think in the end we have to prove it. And you just watch us: we'll get this job done.*

(In this setting, 25 years of experience at GM is a negative, not a positive. He needs to talk about how he has seen the company respond successfully to changes in the past and how he will be a change agent in the future.)

Gregory: *But you can be relied upon to bring change?*

Henderson: *I will spend 100 percent of my time doing exactly that.*

(Again, no specifics, just a promise to work hard. The interview conveys good intentions but no sign of leadership.)[1]

The Preparation Process

There are three components to any interview: preparation, execution, and debriefing. Of these, the most important by far is preparation.

As a communicator, you must make the time to prepare for every interview. Yes, even if you are being interviewed for the thirtieth time on the same subject. Different reporters will approach a subject different ways, and you need to be ready for however they will do it.

The overall procedure for preparation is to analyze both the interviewer and the audience; identify key issues of interest or positions of the interviewer; determine what you want that audience to do, say, think, or feel after the interview; create your three Must Airs; prepare answers for your most difficult questions; and rehearse the interview.

A frequent mistake made by interviewees is trying to make too many points. Remember: communication is not what the speaker knows or says but what the listener takes away. It's best to pick three headline points with proofs or examples to back them up. Why only three? Because you can remember three, and so can the journalist and the audience. Beyond three, you're pushing it.

You may have 100 good points. But if you try to make all of them, you are taking a chance on what a print reporter puts into his story or what the person watching the interview on TV takes away. Keeping it to three Must Airs, with suitable subpoints is the best course for winning with the media.

Let's look at each step of the preparation process:

- **Analyze the interviewer and the audience.** Is this a business reporter, a general reporter, or someone who specializes in your industry? Is it someone who has a particular interest in or bias about your company or your industry? You will create different Must Airs for and expect different questions from each. Who will be watching this interview or reading or hearing this story, what portion of that group do you want to target, and what do you want to say to them? How will the interview be used: live, excerpted, long-form magazine story, or something else?

- **Determine what you want that audience to do, say, think, or feel after the interview.** How do you want them to perceive you and your organization as a result of this interview? Once you decide this, you can move on to the next step.
- **Create your three Must Airs.** As I said before, Must Airs are short, declarative, provable sentences fashioned to convince your audience to respond as you want them to. Creating your Must Airs is the hardest and most important part of the preparation process.

  One method I've used to help my clients come up with their Must Airs is to have executives list all the major positives about their company or organization. Once you have a good working list, we look for three sentences or areas that add up to the perception we want.

  It is critical that the Must Airs be worded as strongly as possible. These are the *exact words* you want to say on the air. We want to go as far as we can while still being 100 percent truthful. For example, while "We have five products that are performing well" is an okay Must Air, "We have three of the top five brands in the United States" is stronger.

  You should also create subpoints for your Must Airs. These should be facts that back-up the Must Air, while still meeting the criteria of short, declarative, and provable. For the example in the previous paragraph, a good subpoint could be "Macho Cologne is tops among men 18 to 25."

  While the points must be delivered as planned, they must be phrased in natural, conversational tones and not sound like they were prerecorded.

  Associated Press business reporter Joyce Rosenberg says she finds no fault with an executive delivering a planned message as long as that person is also straightforward and responsive to her questions. But, she notes, "Executives too often sound scripted," she says. "They speak in platitudes. Also, they are too often not prepared or willing to discuss key issues."

  Her advice is to be "honest, open, and flexible," which sounds exactly like the advice we give.

  Proper rehearsal, with the questions coming in several different forms, can help remove that scripted feeling.
- **Prepare answers for your most difficult questions.** Potential negative questions should be identified, and bottom-line answers prepared. Start by picking the three where your position is weakest or most likely to be challenged, and then expand to include any others you may face. Remember that a tough question can come out of a perception of your company that is not true. So you need to be prepared to counter the false perception and point out your positives in that area, as well as being prepared to address genuine mistakes, faults, and weaknesses.

- **Rehearse the interview.** If you are not having a full media training session prior to the interview (see Chapter 13, "Media Training: A Modern Day Necessity"), ask someone from your communications team to play the role of the reporter and simulate the interview. Video record the simulation (or audio if it's a phone interview) and have both of you critique your performance. Not only does this improve your performance, it also helps you field test your Must Airs. Sometimes a Must Air that sounds great at the drawing board falls apart when it's actually used in an interview. It's best to find this out in rehearsal and not in front of a live TV camera.

The "Cosmetics" of Being Interviewed

While crafting and delivering the right messages is the most important part of an interview, the physical or "cosmetic" aspects cannot be ignored.

In our training, we focus on TV interviews because for the most part they require the tightest answers and cause the most anxiety. Also, I have found that the lessons from TV interviews are easier to carry over to other media (radio, print, email) than vice versa. So, while most of the points I will make here are about TV, they do apply to other media as well.

The most important thing in a TV interview is eye contact. Remember, it is critical for you to have credibility when being interviewed, and eye contact is key to that credibility. You should look your interviewer in the eye (unless otherwise instructed, for example at the beginning of the interview) and not at the camera. This is even more important when you are asked a tough question. Looking at the floor, the ceiling, or off to the left or right when you are hit with a challenging question makes you appear evasive, or even dishonest. If you are a little uncomfortable looking directly in your interviewer's eyes, look at his or her nose, between the eyebrows, or somewhere in that vicinity so it appears you are looking him or her in the eye.

You should start your interview with a nice smile unless the topic you are discussing is so serious that it would appear insensitive to be smiling. Remember, you are glad to be there. You are getting the chance to tell your story, and if you are facing a hostile interviewer, having a smile on your face tells the audience you are confident in your position and can handle even the toughest question.

Gestures are great. Gestures make you look more interesting. They help your voice have energy and emphasis, and they make you more believable. Gestures signify passion and involvement. Try to find a couple of interviews on television for a comparison: one with a newsmaker gesturing and one devoid of gestures. You'll see a significant difference in the impression of conviction and sincerity that is conveyed.

On TV, your hand gestures should be up around your shoulders in what I call "TV range." That way, even if you are on a pretty tight shot, your hands will still be seen.

The gesture should not be elaborate; we're not talking about painting pictures with your hands or an interpretive dance about your topic. What you want is a simple movement of one or both of your hands from next to your shoulders to slightly away from them, using your elbows as the fulcrum. Keep your fingers together; splayed fingers call attention to themselves and distract from your point.

In terms of posture, you want to be sitting up straight, not slouching in the chair. When you sit down, don't go all the way to the back of the seat; sit about three-quarters of the way back. Then make a fist and place it in the small of your back. Lean back until your fist hits the seat back. Then remove your fist and stay in that same position. This will make you appear alert and interested and will prevent you from leaning back or looking defensive when you are asked a tough question.

When you are not gesturing, have your hands resting on the arms of the chair or on your legs, not in your lap. Your legs should be spread about as far apart as your hips, neither opened nor closed. Crossing your legs is usually not recommended for men, but crossing them at the ankles tends to work well for women.

It is a good idea to use the reporter's name unless you are specifically told not to. This helps build a bridge between you two and makes the audience feel that this is a conversation between equals, not an inquisition or trial. Using the reporter's name also gives you a little time to phrase your answer perfectly. "Ted, while that has been a problem in the past, we now see a trend toward. . . ."

Often when you are interviewed you will be asked for a sound check so the technician can set voice levels. Most people in this circumstance will say "Testing, 1, 2, 3. Is this on?" What I tell executives to do in this circumstance is to say (1) your name, (2) your title and affiliation, and (3) one of your Must Airs. For example, when asked for a sound check you can say, "Hello, I'm David Lang, CEO of Beethoven Industries, and I'm here to talk about how we are introducing three new products that will revolutionize the aerospace industry." This puts your prime point in your interviewer's mind, and you might even find him leading off the interview with "You are about to announce products that you say will revolutionize the aerospace industry. Tell us about them." You are already on "your side of the page" before you have even said a word.

In terms of dress and clothing, it should match your position, situation, and industry, as I discussed in Chapter 2, "You Are a Brand: Make It the Right One." When appearing on TV, it is important that your clothing, jewelry, and accessories not distract from your message. Anything that stands out, like long dangling earrings, a bright lapel pin, or vibrant shirt or jacket, should be left home. We want the audience to focus on your message, not your clothes (unless you are the CEO of a clothing manufacturer, of course).

And, last, TV absorbs energy. You have to bring some good, positive energy with you when you appear on the air. That doesn't mean "hype" or exaggerated or outlandish behavior. Just a good, solid amount of energy, as when giving a speech.

As I said before, almost all of these tips work for non-TV interviews as well. For example, you should still gesture and have good eye contact when meeting face-to-face with a print reporter, and you should absolutely use the reporter's name.

The News Conference

At some point in your career you may find yourself holding a news conference. While these are less common today, there are still times when the head of an organization has to go before the gathered media, make a brief statement, and handle questions.

The most obvious example is during a crisis (see Chapter 21). When a situation gets bad enough, the CEO has to go out there and explain the situation, what the company is doing about it, and what the impact is.

News conferences are also used to announce good news, such as the opening of a new facility or the successful completion of a charity drive or other program. If one of your holdings is a sports team, you may be on hand to announce the hiring of a new coach or general manager.

You and your PR team can determine when to hold a news conference. Here's how to make it successful.

Your preparation is pretty much the same as for any interview. Select your Must Air points and the answers to your most difficult questions.

Then you and your team should write a short statement about your situation. How short? That depends on the circumstances, but in almost no cases should the statement be longer than three to five minutes. This statement is based around your Must Airs, tells the details of the situation, and does not speculate (especially in crisis).

After reading the statement (using the good speech delivery techniques in Chapter 15, "Winning at the Lectern"), tell the media that you have some time for questions. It's often a good idea to set a time limit on questions, but try to see that everybody present gets to ask at least one.

As you get each question, use the Satisfy-and-Steer technique outlined earlier in this chapter. You will find this section of the news conference operates much like a standard interview. The biggest difference, however, is that because you will be taking questions from a number of people there will be less of a linear flow to the conversation. It is less likely that the question you face will have come directly out of your last answer because the questioner is *likely* to be interested in a different aspect of the story.

When you take a question from a member of the media, start by looking straight at that person. Then, as you answer, move your eyes toward another reporter and let that person ask the next question. This allows you to spread your gaze around the room and doesn't turn your Q&A session into a one-on-one interview.

This is especially helpful if that reporter asked you a particularly difficult question. By moving your eyes to someone else, you have limited the opportunity for that reporter to hit you with an even tougher follow-up. Of course, with your preparation you would have handled it smoothly anyway; but why invite trouble?

The Ambush Interview

It strikes fear in the heart of the strongest and most confident executive: the ambush interview. You come around the corner and there they are—media demons with smirking looks and evil grins, jamming cameras and microphones in your face and demanding answers to the hardest questions. Is there any way you can look good in this situation?

Yes, there is. Even this seemingly one-sided battle can be won.

Ambush interviews by major media occur less frequently these days because of staff cutbacks, but they are not unheard of, especially in countries like the United Kingdom where "gotcha" journalism is an art form.

Why do they happen? Very simply because the reporters are being stonewalled on important issues. I always tell my clients, "There should never be an ambush interview. If your public relations arm operates with honesty and transparency, giving the public the important facts and appropriate comment, there is nothing to ambush. They will have your story, so they will move on to someone and something else."

A favorite venue for an ambush interview is the courthouse steps. Another place reporters lurk is just outside hearing rooms. Someone who has been on the griddle for the last two hours should be easy pickin's for an ambush pro.

Shed your victim hat and put on your leader hat.

The worst thing you can do is pull your jacket up over your head, barrel through the crowd, and race to your car or into your office. I guarantee you that will appear on the news, and everyone who sees it will assume you are guilty.

Instead, when you see the media, if you aren't prepared at that moment, greet them with a friendly "Hello!" If you're not sure of the reason they're there, ask what the story is, and then either give them your prepared response or tell them you'll hold a briefing in a few minutes to provide the answers. Then do so. Once again, and you'll probably grow tired of hearing this from me before you finish this book, the secret is preparation, along with maintaining your leader presence.

Courtrooms and hearing rooms are sanctuaries; eager reporters are not likely to assault you there. So, in those surroundings, take a minute when your testimony is finished before exiting the room, and prepare your Must Air points. Also, prepare answers for the toughest questions, including anything new that may have come up in the hearing or trial. When you walk out into the storm, take the first question, satisfy it, and steer to your points. Take immediate control and maintain it, just as you would in a business interview in a more sedate setting.

This encounter does not have to last long. After you've made your points and answered just a few questions, feel free to say "thank you" and walk away. Unless you've dodged some critical question or issue, you're not likely to be pursued.

Your control of the situation is going to make you look good on television that night. People will see a leader who faced a challenging situation, dealt with it successfully, and walked away with his dignity and reputation intact.

You won.

Is It Worth It?

Winning in the media is not easy. It takes dedication, thought, a process, and practice, practice, practice. Is it worth it?

Of course it is. Ignoring for a second the dangers of handling the media poorly, successful media appearances enhance the image of the company and the executive.

A solid PR team can use your good interviews to attract more customers, promote the company, and get you invited to better and more prestigious speaking and media engagements. A CEO who shows he can handle tough questions is seen as a dynamic leader who can steer the company through its roughest seas. With more and more websites and TV networks needing video, you can position yourself before millions of people as a strong leader of a good organization.

Tips

- Regard the news media as an outlet for your story, not an enemy.
- Prepare your Must Air points carefully and illustrate them with examples.
- Prepare concise and direct responses to all difficult or negative questions.
- Satisfy and steer the discussion to your agenda.
- Don't panic if you're unexpectedly confronted by reporters; take control.
- Pay attention to such "cosmetics" as eye contact, posture, and gestures.

Note

1. *Meet the Press* on NBC, April 5, 2009. Full transcript: http://www.msnbc.msn.com/id/30055730/ns/meet_the_press/t/meet-press-transcript-april/#.T7vB68X4L3Y.

CHAPTER 13

Media Training: A Modern Day Necessity

"It is utter folly to put anyone in front of the media without media training."

—Dick Kulp, lead trainer, Virgil Scudder & Associates, and former NBC newscaster

Like so many things that have blossomed into standard corporate practice, media training had humble beginnings.

It reportedly got started in the 1970s when the CEO of a large company went to his advertising agency and said, "I need help. I have a big television interview coming up, and I have no idea about how to handle it."

So two agency executives did a quick study of good and bad interviews, put together a training program for him, and grilled him on camera. He did well in the subsequent interview, and an industry was born.

Today, media training is global and is a staple of virtually every business of any size. It's a must for CEOs.

One of my clients has a firm policy: no one is permitted to go before the media without first undergoing media training. That policy includes everybody in the C-suite and the company's very capable corporate communications staff.

Governments of countries large and small utilize media training; so does the military. So do charities, and even organizations that have no immediate plan to put their employees in front of the cameras and microphones.

Why?

Because the training not only prepares the person for planned or unplanned media encounters; it teaches a discipline that carries over into many other areas.

Principles of Media Training

But even to this day, media training is often misunderstood. Some think of it as charm school, others a test of their knowledge of the subject. Some see it as bag of tricks, a system of deception.

I've heard journalists say, "I don't want to talk to anyone who has been media trained. They won't give you straight answers."

If that's true, that person has not been properly trained. Good media training does not counsel evasion because, as we noted in Chapter 12, evasion destroys a person's credibility, and credibility is essential to success in presenting an argument.

As you'll note in the previous chapter, at no time did I counsel any kind of evasion or deception. I stress the following principle in dealing with the media or anyone else: never lie, deceive, or mislead. It will come back to haunt you someday. However, this principle does not mean that you should immediately start spewing out all of your dirty laundry.

Here's a real-life example of that from a celebrity whom I once trained for the media tour to promote her autobiography.

The woman had been divorced, and I noticed in reading through the book that she referred to the failed marriage but never identified her ex-husband by name. I thought that was unusual and asked her why.

"He's a glory hound," she responded. "If his name is in it, he'll be out in front of book stores signing autographs and waving to cameras. I don't want to see that."

So our task was to come up with points that would be truthful but not go into that kind of detail. When she was asked why his name wasn't in the book, she was to reply:

- As is well known, it was a bitter divorce that I'm trying to put behind me.
- I only mentioned it because it was a turning point in my career.
- I did not feel his name was essential to what I had to say.

The strategy worked. No journalist probed beyond the immediate response.

It also helped that she would then immediately steer the conversation to another topic with words like "One of the stories I recount in the book is when. . . ."

Preparing for Positives and Negatives

A key element of media training is condensing a lot of information into the most important elements of the story and developing points that are immediately and easily understood. The training shows people how to get a message across clearly on a topic that may be complex, confusing, or controversial.

If media training is done right and there is proper follow-up, there should never be a negative question that catches the executive by surprise.

Since the prime goal of media training is a smooth and effective interview with no surprises, it's essential that the negatives be brought up and proper answers prepared. Sometimes you'll find that what appeared to be a negative is really a positive.

This situation arose when I was training the CEO of a timber company in Borneo, East Malaysia. When I asked him what negatives he might face, he said, "There is one that could come up, but I don't want to talk about it." I told him that, if I were to help him with an answer, I would need to hear what it was.

His response was not surprising: water pollution. Timber and paper companies necessarily pollute streams; there is no disputing that point, but I knew we had to go a step further to help him prepare an answer. So I asked him if his company was the worst in the industry in terms of water pollution. "No," he replied. "We are one of the more responsible ones."

Then I asked if the company was making any efforts to reduce the pollution and, if so, was it getting any results. "Oh, yes," he said, beaming. "We've cut it nearly 50 percent over the last 5 years."

So an apparent negative was really a hidden positive that could be used whenever the company was challenged on its environmental record. I told him he shouldn't bring up the subject during an interview about timber output or the company's financial prospects, but it certainly could be a plus in other situations. If the company chose to do a program on corporate responsibility, here was a prime example for starters.

Uses Outside of Media Interviews

The discipline of condensing and refining messages in media training has widespread uses. The head of one organization said that the system of message development that she took from our media training sessions became the model for her organization in preparing for government hearings, staff meetings, investor meetings, and a host of others.

"The system works," she said, "going in with a key theme, three headline points, and clear examples and proofs to back up those points, followed by identifying and providing clear, concise responses to all potential negatives."

Simple, direct communication is powerful.

Obviously, I was aware of these various applications, but I came across one that surprised me. I was in Washington, D.C., media training a lawyer who was about to make an argument before the United States Supreme

Court. Because I am not a lawyer, I had nothing to contribute to that, or so I thought. My job was to prepare him for the courthouse-steps interviews that would inevitably follow the high-profile hearing. He had to condense his extensive argument before the court to three solid Must Airs for reporters.

When we finished the training, he surprised me. He said, "You know, I've been thinking about my court presentation, and I think I can apply some of these techniques to it. Yes, clear, concise, credible. My presentation hasn't fully gotten to that standard yet, and it needs to."

I wasn't there for the court testimony, but I suspect these techniques made it a bit better. Clarity is never out of fashion.

Devote Enough Time to Training

CEOs guard their time jealously, and they must, but it is a mistake not to allow time for media training when millions of people will see and judge a person's presence and performance.

How much time is needed to do it right? I recommend a day of one-on-one training for a corporate head initially, with refreshers prior to major appearances.

The head of public relations of an international consulting firm felt her CEO needed to be more visible, but he had had no previous training and little media experience. She was naturally afraid to schedule media interviews without some indication that he would do well in them, so she convinced him to spend some time with me.

He said he would do two hours of training; that's all the time he could spare. I turned him down. He was shocked. I told his aide that I did not believe that we could cover all the things that needed to be covered and come up with the right responses to the most difficult negatives in that limited time period, and I refused to send him out on media appearances without more preparation. He relented and carved out a bigger time slot for the training. It was time well spent.

CEOs of the biggest firms should always be trained one-on-one. The size of the training group can grow as you move down the ranks, but even at the vice presidential level we try to hold the ratio to four people to one trainer. The participants need to have enough time to practice the techniques and master the "satisfy and steer" process.

One challenge that media trainers face is that those at the top are accustomed to hearing praise, not critical analysis. Not many people have the courage to tell the boss that he or she handled questions badly or failed to make the company's case in an interview. When I told one CEO that he needed to improve his technique, he replied, "Really? My secretary says I'm quite good at this." Overcoming the in-house cheering squad requires some diplomacy, but a well-critiqued review of the first interview will usually bring reality to the process.

Communication skills, like any other learned behavior, can erode if not used or practiced. Periodic brush-up sessions, say every 6 to 12 months, are always a good idea, and a media training–style rehearsal should be scheduled before every major interview or series of interviews.

Finding the Right Trainer

Picking a media trainer for the boss is hard. The trainer–executive relationship is highly personal in nature. The two must interact on a level of mutual respect. The trainer must have sufficient experience and gravitas to be taken seriously, and teaching style is important: the trainer's critiques must be honest but polite.

A good training program needs to include developing and/or refining messages, an orientation to dealing with the media, identification of key points to stress about the company or topic, preparation of effective answers for tough questions, vocal and physical technique, and several practice interviews with video recording and playback.

It is important that the media trainer be told all the "dirty laundry" that could conceivably come up in an interview. That means that there must be a trust level between the trainer and the CEO. The trainer should also be willing to sign a confidentiality agreement and understand the seriousness of that agreement.

A public relations officer once told me, "I want you to get our boss ready for media interviews, but don't ask him any tough questions." I responded that the only way I could, or would, do that is if I were assured that no journalist would ask him any hard questions. That can never be assured.

People who rise to the top of an organization welcome challenge. They need and want to be confronted with the most difficult questions and issues and shown how to navigate successfully through them. Easy, sugar-coated training that avoids tackling such issues leaves the executive vulnerable to a disastrous real-world experience.

The CEO's Media Training Session

What should go into a one-day program for a C-level executive? The elements should be tailored to the needs and experience of the individual, but I would generally include television, radio, and print interviews, a telephone interview, and perhaps a crisis news briefing exercise. Such a day is jam-packed and intense, but people who rise to the top are used to working hard all day and being put under pressure. It is better to overprepare than under-prepare.

Success in the media basically relies on two things: preparation and technique. Preparation is an ongoing process; technique is learned and practiced.

Like any skill, communication technique can erode over time if not regularly used. As I said before, even the best media communicators should get a brush-up every 6 to 12 months. This could require only two or three hours, and it's a good investment of that time.

In sum, media training is here to stay. Those who master the system and the techniques have a distinct advantage over those who do not. This is a process that no CEO or anyone who aspires to leadership should neglect or avoid.

Tips

- Consider media training essential to personal and corporate success.
- Select a trainer with broad knowledge and experience who will challenge the executive and company positions.
- Be sure the chemistry between the trainer and the executive is right.
- Allocate sufficient time for the training.
- Conduct a media training–style rehearsal before every major public appearance.
- Apply media training preparation techniques to other communication situations.
- Repeat the training periodically so the lessons stick.

PART IV

Public Appearances

CHAPTER 14

Public Speaking: Power, Persuasion, and Good Will

"Speechmaking is one of the most effective and powerful ways to project yourself as the leader that you are and the leader that you hope to be."

—Dana Rubin, founder-director, New York Speechwriters Roundtable

Think back to the 1990s, when the "digital age" was really getting rolling. Some people, who prided themselves on an ability to see into the future, made a number of forecasts: we would become a paperless society in the 2000s, face-to-face conversation would largely become passé—replaced by universal use of video—and one of our biggest problems would be what to do with all of the free time the digital revolution would bring us.

Perhaps those futurists should have heeded the advice of old-time movie mogul Samuel Goldwyn: "Never make forecasts, especially about the future."

Face-to-Face Still Matters

In spite of wonders like email, instant messaging, and texting, many companies still seem to be heavily laden with paper. Face-to-face conversation is obviously not dead; in fact, for a leader, it may be more important than ever, and most executives seem to have less free time than ever.

In my experience, few executives look forward to delivering a speech, but public speaking is a critical tool for those who lead or wish to lead.

There are many benefits to addressing the right audiences with the right message. Public appearances allow the speaker to define and lead the conversation on an issue, to promote a company's policies or product line, and to establish the individual and the company as the standard for the industry.

Both the organization and the individual benefit from a well-planned, well-executed approach to public speaking.

James C. Humes, speechwriter for Presidents Eisenhower, Nixon, Ford, and Reagan, once noted, "Every time you have to speak, you are auditioning for leadership."

I'd go a step further: every time you speak, you are demonstrating, or failing to demonstrate, leadership.

While the Humes comment applies to all speakers, I would particularly recommend that young executives take note of it. As legendary news broadcaster Lowell Thomas once said, "The man who can speak acceptably is generally given credit for an ability all out of proportion to what he really possesses." Obviously, the point is no less true for women, and no less true today than when it was uttered more than half a century ago.

The Power of Public Speaking

While the growth of electronics has added new ways for us to communicate, public speaking (with the exception of such tools as teleprompters and PowerPoint) looks very much like it has for centuries, and the connection between strong public speaking skills and business success has never been greater.

Public appearances are especially important for a CEO. The CEO is the personification of the company, but other high-level executives can play an important role in the company's success with solid performances at the lectern.

A classic example of the power of public speaking comes from UPS. In the late 1990s, the company was growing fast and taking a leadership position in its field. Its profile was quickly changing from a shipping company to a leader in logistics. It planned to go public after a century as a privately held firm and needed to tell its story to a new set of stakeholders.

Public appearances by the CEO and other key executives were a major part of the plan. Steve Soltis, who was brought in to lead the company's executive communication department, told me, "Our primary goal was to tell our growth story and reinforce to investors, media, employees, and other stakeholders that we had a clear vision for growth and an extremely talented leadership team to guide us."

The program began rolling in earnest in 1997. It involved not only the chairman and CEO but also the vice chairman, the chief operating officer, and the heads of marketing, human resources, and international business.

By 1999, Soltis's department was producing in excess of 70 speeches a year for the executive team. They were delivered before the most prestigious audiences, and the material developed for the talks was widely marketed well beyond the day of the event.

The program paid off royally, says Soltis. "We got tremendous media exposure and peer exposure. It positioned our folks as thought leaders and ambassadors for the brand, and it helped make a historically 'quiet and somewhat shy company' much more extroverted and seemingly transparent."

Among the results of this increased visibility were business magazine cover stories, selection as a *Fortune* "most admired company," and the success of the largest IPO in history.

Said Soltis, "I would not say that public speaking led to the cover story, but it certainly helped raise the profile of our executives and, in particular, our CEO, Jim Kelly. Most of these folks could count on one hand the number of external public speeches that had been given prior to the launch of the program."

It is a mistake to think that the impact of a speech must end when a high-level speaker sits down. A lot of time and effort goes into the speech, and a lot should come out of it. There are numerous places where the text and video can be posted to bring the message to a wider audience, including new avenues in social media. For example, your CEO's best appearances should be recorded and posted on your company's YouTube channel and Facebook page. Then you can tweet a link to the talk from the company's Twitter feed.

Once again, the UPS campaign provides us with a good example of the reach of a talk. The occasion of a speech by CEO James Kelly at Town Hall, Los Angeles, was turned into over 26 million impressions by the company's public relations arm. Kelly did media interviews in connection with the talk, and an AP story alone reached millions of readers. The content was also turned into op-ed articles, posted on the Internet and Intranet, and distributed through reprints, among other things.

Kelly's willingness to make that speech in Los Angeles led to a huge bonanza for the company in terms of prestige, recognition, and good will.

Use the Pile Driver

An effective speech has to be highly focused and limited in how much it tries to cover. There should be a clear main theme followed by a limited number of points.

Winston Churchill put it this way: "If you have an important point to make, don't try to be subtle or clever. Use the pile driver. Hit the point once. Then, come back and hit it again. Then hit it a third time: a tremendous whack."

When Churchill talked, people listened, and they remembered, even decades later.

Some might question the value of investing the time and cost of preparing and delivering a good speech. After all, there are many ways to reach people through electronic communication.

But Dana Rubin, veteran executive speechwriter and founder-director of the New York Speechwriters Roundtable, says, "The different media reach very different audiences. There is a large portion of the population—people who are very influential—who don't read tweets or have time for Facebook, but they do attend conferences because they know that those are the places where they are going to meet and hear from just the kind of people that are key influencers."

Thought leadership speeches should be a part of every CEO's management plan. Says Rubin, "They are a way of projecting eminence or preeminence in the marketplace. It puts the individual in the role of being a high-level thinker. It's not only of service to the individual but also the organization the individual represents."

For a CEO, well-chosen public speaking appearances are part of the job. It's no longer a question of whether. It's when, where, how often, and for what purpose. The proper attitude and proper preparation for speeches will offer benefits not just the day of the talk, but for months to come, and those traits go a long way toward establishing the CEO as a corporate and thought leader.

Tips

- Consider public speaking an essential part of your job responsibilities.
- Look for forums and topics that will position you and your company in a leadership role.
- Be sure your talk is focused on a limited number of points.
- Consider ways that the material developed for the talk can be used in other venues.

CHAPTER 15

Winning at the Lectern

"I do not object to people looking at their watches when I am speaking. But I strongly object when they start shaking them to make sure they are still working."

—*William Norman Birkett, British lawyer and judge*

If you want to see true pain, watch the face of a speechwriter whose boss is standing before a group, droning and mumbling his way through some of the best material the scribe ever wrote.

Most CEOs aren't terrible public speakers or they wouldn't have gotten to where they are, but there are also few who can give James Earl Jones a run for his money.

But, you may say, "Jones is an actor. Public speaking comes naturally to him." I don't think so.

Good speakers are made, not born. True, some have more aptitude for it than others, some have better voices, and some have a more innate sense of language, but nobody is born with it any more than the great soprano Renée Fleming was born hitting the high Cs. (Or Ds, or whatever it is that great sopranos hit.)

Ronald Reagan was both an actor and an outstanding public speaker. No one questions that his skill at public speaking played a big role in propelling him to the White House, but Reagan worked hard at developing his podium talent. There are many good actors who are terrible when they get up in front of a crowd. Have you seen the Oscars lately? Some of the best actors of the day would finish in the second division in an oratorical competition.

Look at what public speaking skills did for President Barack Obama. Obama was a junior senator from Illinois when he spoke at the 2004 Democratic national convention. He was such a secondary player that his speech wasn't even carried on network television. You had to tune in to PBS to see it.

But he electrified the crowd, and suddenly he was being talked about as a future president.

I find that most high-level executives, even CEOs, struggle with making a scripted speech come to life. Many people who are excellent at PowerPoint or speaking off the cuff lose their edge when handed written material that must be delivered word-for-word.

Delivering a scripted speech effectively requires practice, discipline, and learning some tricks of the trade. If it is done right, the audience will swear that the speaker wrote the speech, and that's what it needs to sound like.

Many things contribute to success when a great speaker steps up to the lectern. Invariably, he or she is ready—well-rehearsed, well-rested, and fully familiar with the material. Under-rehearsing is the biggest single complaint I hear speechwriters voice about their corporate bosses.

The material must be good—skillfully written and relevant to the audience—and the delivery must be authoritative.

Speakers can learn a lot from singers, especially those in the operatic world. Listen to someone like Renée Fleming or Thomas Hampson. Their voices will rise and fall, from very loud to very soft, as their words tell a story in music. Obviously, the pitch will vary, and so will the pace. Some passages will be sped up, and some slowed down. There will be pauses, known as rests, that will add impact to what the performer is trying to convey in song.

Good speakers use exactly the same techniques. It is primarily the variation of the voice, along with clear, well-modulated delivery, that makes the great speakers great. Sameness is boring, and too many speakers are captive to it.

Public speaking is a form of acting. It frightens some executives when I say that. They'll say, "I don't want to be some phony actor; I want to be me." My answer is, "I don't want you to be anybody but you, but I want you to be the most powerful and authoritative you that you can be."

An actor is not "phony." An actor is an interpreter. So is a public speaker. Both bring words to life and shape them to have meaning.

Variety Is the Spice of Speaking

So, if variation is the key, what should be varied? The list includes pace, pitch, volume, and even pauses. Yes, even varying the length of your pauses can add impact to a speech.

Pace

We'll start with pace, the first step on the speaker's journey to greatness. A speaker whose pace is too fast or too slow cannot achieve the expressiveness needed to move or inspire an audience. Getting the pace right is the first step. Once the basic pace is right, it should be varied from time to time, speeding up slightly on a less important passage, and slowing down when a key point is being made.

Pitch

While most executives are not monotones, most could use more variation in pitch. Reach for the high notes on occasion and dig for the low notes.

Volume

Changes in volume are the hardest thing to teach most business speakers, but they are one of the most effective techniques we have. Use a classic actor or a great singer as a model. Listen to how often they will go from a soft passage to a booming declaration. You are moved, and while your material might not be as dramatic as the dialogue in *King Lear*, the principle is the same: varying the volume adds greatly to the impact of a speech.

Pauses

Pauses are the neglected stepsister of public speaking. Too many speakers will zip from one sentence to another, hesitating only to grab a breath every few sentences or so. Such a speaker is hard to follow, and an audience will quickly tune out.

When should the speaker pause? For starters, every punctuation mark calls for a pause. A move from one section of a talk to another calls for a pause. There are also pauses for effect. A pause made after an important statement underlines that statement. A pause after asking a question gives the audience a chance to think about it. It's a good idea to pause after delivering a number because the ear and the brain don't work too well at absorbing numbers.

Too many speakers don't get better because they don't listen to themselves speaking. However, once they see and hear themselves on video in our studios, they often express surprise. "I thought I was better than that," they'll say. Sorry, but the cameras and microphones don't lie. But I tell them, "You can get better pretty quickly if you'll devote some time to practice and apply these techniques." Remember what I said earlier: speakers are made, not born. Anyone who is willing to work at it can become a good speaker.

Charting where you are is the first step to growth. Stop, if you can, right now (or as soon as you can) and grab a part of a speech script and an audio recorder. Practice the things I've listed—varying the pace, pitch, volume, and pauses—and you'll see an immediate effect.

Physicalities of Speaking

Now let's talk about some of the physical aspects of delivering a speech. First impressions are always important, and your first impression should be of someone smiling and walking confidently up to the lectern. Start with burst of energy—a vigorous "good morning" or "good evening" instead of a subdued one. That energy is contagious and it will prime the audience for an interesting experience.

Eye Contact

Eye contact is critically important, but good eye contact can be difficult when delivering a scripted talk, or even one from a teleprompter. However, there are some ways to overcome the handicap of having to deliver written material, even that with which you are not totally familiar.

An obvious point here is that the better you know the speech, the more eye contact you're likely to make. However, because corporate leaders often don't have or take the time for much rehearsal, other devices have to be relied upon.

The first and most important one has to do with speechwriting. Short sentences or longer sentences that break naturally in to short phrases make eye contact much easier. You'll find more on that in Chapter 16.

For now, try this experiment: deliver the next sentence aloud, looking at a person or object, and maintain as much eye contact and expressiveness as you can:

> *As we saw results in the third and fourth quarters from our operations in Japan, China, Saudi Arabia, and Europe, and as we factored in currency rates, local inflation, and taxation rates, we decided that a move to a more local system of inventory reduction was called for, and we anticipate moving to such a system within the next 180 days.*

Now try it this way:

> *Our operations in Japan, China, Saudi Arabia, and Europe produced good results in the third and fourth quarters. But we see opportunities for further improvement. We've looked at currency rates, local inflation, and taxation rates, and come to this conclusion: we need a local approach to inventory reduction. So, we expect to move to such a system within the next 180 days.*

The second version went a lot better, didn't it? Point made.

Another key to good eye contact is the layout of the material. Pick a font of 24 points or more. Tell the person who prepares your material to put a page number at the upper right of each page, double or triple space between lines, and put only two or three short paragraphs on a page. Also, never have a sentence spill over to the next page.

We recommend margins of top 1″, bottom 3″, and left 2″, and right 1.5″. With big type, a lot of white space, very little on a page, you should be able to maximize your eye contact.

When should you make eye contact? It's most important when you say "I," "we," "you," the name of your organization, or the name of the people or organization you are addressing.

But it's also important when you make your key points and on the key word in each sentence or phrase. Here's something that's hard for many speakers to do but, if you can do it, is very effective: have your eyes up at the beginning and end of each sentence, looking down at your material only between sentences or in the middle of long sentences. It's hard to do but if you accomplish it, you'll look like someone who knows his material inside and out and is only looking down to check a few notes.

Move your eye contact around the room, but not in "windshield wiper" fashion. Deliver a sentence or two to one person, then move to another for a sentence or two, and so on around the room.

Gesturing

Good eye contact makes the speaker seem more authoritative and confident. So do good gestures. A gesture should punctuate every key point in the talk.

What is a good gesture? I recommend a simple directing of the hand toward the person to whom you are speaking. As in the TV interview (Chapter 12, "Winning in the Media"), you want to keep your fingers together. You make your gesture toward the audience, and then rest your hand gently on the lectern until the next gesture.

Use your right hand when speaking to your right, left hand when speaking to your left, and either or both hands when speaking to the middle. You don't want to "cross" yourself; if you gesture with your right hand to the left side of the audience, you are effectively blocking the right side of the audience from seeing your face. Using the correct hand makes you and your body language more open.

Gestures and eye contact are tightly related. Your eyes and your hand *must* go together. If you are gesturing to the right, you must be looking to the right. This prevents confusion in the audience: "Am I supposed to look at his hand or his eyes?"

Also, you cannot gesture while you are looking down at your page.

Some speakers remind me of an old Western movie where our hero has his head down behind a rock with his pistol hoisted above shooting over it. He'll never hit anything, and the speaker who emulates that Western hero by burying his head in his script won't score much with an audience, either.

Interpreting and Flavoring

The final trick of the great speakers is that they interpret and flavor everything they say. If something is good, you should make it sound good by the way you say it, uplifting your voice and raising your pitch. If it is bad, make it sound bad by darkening your voice and lowering your pitch.

The goal is to have your audience understand how you feel about everything you are saying. Much of any business speech is open to interpretation. Is an increase of 3 percent great or terrible? It is up to the speaker to give that number context. You do that through language, of course (up *only* 3 percent), but you can also do it through vocal interpretation.

Numbers often need to be put in perspective. Is the number three a large one or a small one? If you scored a three on a scale of 10, it's awful. But, if you posted a three on a scale of 3, it's a moment for jubilation.

Try this using an audio recorder. Say the numbers 3, 5, 7, and 10. Try to make each one sound good, then make it sound bad. Playing back the recording will give you a measure of the quality of your interpretive technique.

If you get good enough at it, you will be able to convey some meaning to an audience that speaks little or no English or whatever language you are speaking in. They will get some idea of what you mean or how you feel about a subject just by the way you are saying it.

Again using an audio recorder, try delivering the following words in a way that will make them sound like what they mean.

GOOD
BAD
POWERFUL
SAD
EXCITING
DISAPPOINTING
WONDERFUL

If they all sounded the same, you've got work to do. If your interpretation gave some sense of what the words mean, you're on your way to becoming a great speaker.

Now apply the technique to your next speech. Look for these and other "flavor" words and give them the treatment they deserve. Better still, be sure that flavor words are written into all of your speeches.

Regard the Turtle

That's a phrase a business friend of mine loved to use in encouraging people to take risks.

The full quote is "Regard the turtle. He gets nowhere until he sticks his neck out."

I would apply that saying to speakers. Some are so locked in to old habits that it's hard to get them to let their hair down and try something new or something that doesn't "feel right." But we all know that growth in any endeavor is limited if we don't stretch ourselves.

One of the biggest challenges of a speaking coach is to get the executive to take a chance—to try humor, or to vary the volume of his voice, and often, to use gestures. People fear looking or sounding foolish and it can take some persuasion to bring them around. But the combination of a supportive but persistent coach and video playback can usually get the job done.

Every high-level executive has been speaking for a long time. Habits are ingrained, both good ones and bad ones, and we all know that old habits are hard to change.

Here's an exercise I use to show executives how to vary their volume, one that you can use at home. I write the numbers 1 to 5 on a wall chart. Then I ask them to speak each number aloud as I point to it, one being the softest, and five being the loudest, without letting their pitch rise as they get to the higher numbers. It takes some practice, but it works.

Yes, they are practically whispering on number 1 and shouting on number 5. But it shows the speaker just how much variation in volume can be achieved with practice.

I first have them go up the scale from 1 to 5, then down from 5 to 1. The numbers all sound pretty much alike at first, but as they continue practicing the drill and listening to the playback, significant differences begin to show up. Once some variety has been achieved, it's time to apply the technique to a brief section of a speech. Mark each sentence with the number that represents the volume you want to apply. Audio-record your voice with both the number exercise and the speech segment, and I think you'll hear a significant difference.

Why is varying the volume so important? Because it makes the talk sound more interesting and the speaker sound more involved. Raising or lowering your volume causes an audience to listen more intently. Public speaking is interpretation—a form of acting, as I said before—and variation of volume is essential to becoming a great speaker.

Is it done randomly? Of course not, and it's not done on every sentence. Mostly, we use volume variations on key points. Raising or lowering your volume on a key point will cause the audience to pay closer attention and make them more likely to retain the point.

This technique was put to good use recently at the groundbreaking for a large new manufacturing facility in Sumter, South Carolina. The speaker was the CEO for the Americas of a global company, a German native who had worked hard to improve his speaking skills and had gotten some excellent results. He had shown me during our training sessions that he wanted to be an outstanding speaker and was willing to take risks to succeed.

So I told him, "It's time to really stick your neck out on this one. It's a happy day; you are bringing hundreds of jobs to an area that desperately needs them. There is no downside here unless you do a hum-drum job. So, let's let your voice reflect the excitement of the occasion."

Governor Nikki Haley and a slew of other state and local officials were going to be on hand. Governor Haley is an upbeat individual who likes to open her talks with "It's a great day in South Carolina!" In fact, she likes that phrase so much that she encourages workers in state offices to answer the telephone with it (most demur, according to my unofficial sources).

So, I suggested that he open with that line and pull out all of the stops. With a big smile on his face, he boomed out, "As Governor Haley likes to say, It's a great day in South Carolina! It's a great day in Sumter! And (lowering his volume) it's a great day for (our company!)" The opening went over big.

Conquering Nervousness

Mark Twain once said, "There are only two types of speakers in the world: (1) the nervous and (2) liars."

By the time a person becomes CEO of a large corporation, the problem of nervousness may be largely in the past, but because this book is also written with tomorrow's CEO in mind, I decided to include this section.

Why do we get nervous? Because we are on display. We're afraid we'll look foolish or make an embarrassing mistake. Also, there is always the lingering fear that haunts even the most successful talk show hosts: will they love me again tonight?

Let me get one thing out of the way right now: if you make a mistake, just correct it and move on. Few people will remember your slip-up if you deliver well overall.

Nervousness is probably the biggest barrier to effective public speaking. You cannot employ the techniques I've listed in this chapter without getting your nerves under control.

Notice that I said "under control," not "eliminated." Some of the best speakers never totally rid themselves of the tendency to be nervous when in front of an audience. Neither do many of the best actors.

Legendary American actress Helen Hayes once said, "I still get butterflies before a performance. The trick is I have taught them to fly in formation."

Another renowned actor, Raymond Burr, told me early in my public relations career that he got nervous before every performance, even when doing a friendly talk show interview with an admiring host.

"It goes away once I start talking," he said, "but it's there until I open my mouth."

I was amazed. Burr had been a star of stage, screen, and television for nearly half a century, yet he still got nervous. The message was clear: if Raymond Burr can be nervous, admit it, and succeed anyway, so can I, and so can my clients.

Comedian Jerry Seinfeld had a humorous take on the problem. Said Seinfeld, "The number one fear in life is public speaking, and the number two fear is death. That means that if you go to a funeral, you're better off in the casket than giving the eulogy."

That's a premise I can't accept, but it makes the point.

Here are some keys to managing nervousness: preparation, practice, attitude, focus, familiarity, and ice-breaking.

If your talk is well prepared and practiced and you are comfortable with the material, you've just eliminated one reason you might be nervous.

The next is attitude. One public appearance does not make or break a career. While you will do everything you can not to fail, even a bad outing can be overcome by better future performances. This talk is important, but it's not likely to be a career breaker.

If you focus on what you're saying and concentrate on making your audience comfortable, the jitters should subside.

Friendly faces in the audience can also be helpful. If you're speaking to an unfamiliar group, try to meet and chat with as many people as you can before your talk.

And last, find a way to break the ice. Humor is an excellent way if you're comfortable with it (see Chapter 18). If not, you could start off with a question that requires a show of hands. That will reassure you that the audience is paying attention and is ready to listen.

A final note: the more often you speak, the more comfortable you'll be in front of an audience. Young executives should go out of their way to find speaking opportunities, including such things as addressing a church or community group.

For veteran CEOs, who invariably have far more speaking engagements offered than they could or should accept, just be sure you block out adequate rehearsal time.

Next Steps

So now you know what the best speakers do that makes them the best. Mastering these techniques can put you on your way to joining them.

The key now is practice, practice, practice. Video record yourself delivering a recent talk, and then analyze it with a trusted staff member. Practice before your next speech (again, video recording it), and look for ways to improve.

Also, it's never a bad idea to call in a presentation trainer before your most important talks.

Tips

- Work to take your public speaking skills to the highest level.
- Use variation in pace, pitch, and pauses.
- Tell your writer to generally keep sentences and phrases short.
- Try to find more time for rehearsal.
- Practice the exercises offered here.
- Regard the turtle: be willing to stick your neck out to get better.
- Use good eye contact and gestures.

CHAPTER 16

Fielding the Questions: Challenge and Opportunity

"An expert knows all the answers—if you ask the right questions."
—Levi Strauss, American businessman

Speech preparation, as I've outlined in the previous chapters, involves analyzing your audience, developing your key points, working with your speechwriter, and rehearsing your talk. But as Yogi Berra said, "It ain't over 'til it's over."

In a public appearance, it ain't over until you're safely out of the building and in the company of close associates.

Many executives like to deliver a speech or presentation and then race for the exits. There are times when that is appropriate. However, the Q&A period can be one of the most important and valuable parts of a public appearance.

The question and answer period that follows a speech or presentation can often be as beneficial (or as damaging) as what was said before.

Why Do Q&A?

The first thing you should determine when you speak is whether you will take questions at the end or not. Under most circumstances, I recommend that you do allow for a Q&A period?. Why? Three reasons:

1. It makes you appear more open to your audience—you want to address their concerns directly and immediately.

2. It allows you to show your knowledge of your topic—you can get away from your prepared comments and talk about anything on your subject.
3. Most importantly, it allows you another opportunity to make your key points.

Taking questions signals openness and brings an audience into a closer relationship with a speaker. It gives people of feeling of "knowing the person" and that, in itself, has great value in how the individual and his company are perceived.

With sufficient preparation, anyone can stand up and deliver a scripted speech. It's when the questions come that the speaker has a real chance to show his knowledge.

The Q&A period has other advantages. It offers an opportunity to go into greater detail on an important topic that might have been shortened in the talk to meet time limitations, and it offers an opportunity to reinforce the speaker's key points.

Taking questions is a form of listening, a key element of successful management. It also is a helpful research tool. A good CEO listener can glean from audience's questions the matters they are most concerned about and incorporate those into his thinking and planning for the future.

But how do you do it?

Preparing for Q&A

Like all other aspects of communication, the secret to success in Q&A is preparation. That means identifying the things most likely to be asked, with emphasis on the most difficult or challenging ones, and having good, concise answers ready.

Much of this preparation, and execution, is like your media interview preparation (see Chapter 12). As with the media, you have worked out your three main points. Now the challenge is to handle the questions and get to your points (as in an interview).

Figure out ahead of time what questions you will most likely face, and have answers prepared for them. These questions will come out of your talk but also from what is going on in your audience's world. I've told you before to think about all communication from the listener's point of view—here it is critical. Think about what is in your talk that your audience might want explained further or might not accept readily, and be ready to discuss it. Also, think about their circumstances and what they could reasonably expect you to know about those circumstances. Those are the questions you need to prepare for.

Next, figure out which questions are unlikely but potentially deadly to you, and come up with answers for those. We believe it's better and easier to come up with the right answer to a tough question at your desk than it is at the lectern with everyone watching you. I call these the "Oh, sh*t!" questions. As in, "Oh, sh*t, they asked me that!" You should never face a reasonable question in a Q&A that you do not already have an answer for. It is part of your job in preparing your talk.

One of the best ways to handle difficult questions is to preempt them. You do that by putting your answers into the body of your script. If you think, for example, that you are going to face questions about your environmental record, and it hasn't been what it should have been, you can put a line or two into the speech to address it. "I know that a lot of people are concerned about our effect on the environment. I am, too. That's why we are conducting a thorough review of our environmental impact, and I expect that we will see results shortly."

If the question comes up in the Q&A session, you can say, "Well, as I said in my talk, we are conducting a review of our environmental program; and here's what we're looking at." You are now in control of the topic and giving good information as well.

Making Your Points in Q&A

Now that you have your answers, how do you get from those tough questions to your key points? Through the technique we called "Satisfy and Steer," which was explained in Chapter 12.

When you are asked a question that cannot be answered by one of your key points, satisfy that question as quickly as you can, then steer to a relevant key point. As I said before, satisfying involves answering the question just deeply enough to give your audience the bottom line. You can steer by using phrases such as "but, keep in mind the most important area is . . ." or "this is also relevant to. . . ." You should satisfy and steer about 60 percent of the time in a typical Q&A session, and you should do it 100 percent of the time when the questions are hostile.

Let's use the example at the end of the previous section. If you get the question "Isn't it true that the EPA has written up your company 200 times for violations?" you satisfy the question with "yes" or "no" (whichever is true). Then, you steer to the point about your new policy.

"Yes, over a long period of time we did have a lot of write-ups, and that is why we are starting the environmental review that I mentioned. This review, by the way, is part of the overall remaking of the company that I outlined in my talk, and I expect that remaking to save us millions of dollars over the next five years."

No one can say that you didn't answer the question, and you have reiterated your key points.

One last thought on making your points: don't talk too much about one thing. Too many CEOs answer questions with the attitude that they must prove they know about every last detail in every last department of their corporation, as well as the industry and entire business world. You don't. Remember the "Headline-Elaborate-Detail" discussion and chart from Chapter 1. Only give as much detail as is necessary to handle the question. This is not a test of your knowledge; this is an opportunity for you to make your points and sway your audience.

Handling the Tough Questioner

There's one in (almost) every crowd: that person who has only shown up to your talk to give you grief. This person hates your guts, hates your company, probably hates the shirt you're wearing, and he or she is going to use this public appearance to prove to everyone there that you are the worst person on the planet.

How do you handle this person?

One way is to use your eyes as a cueing device. When you take a question from an audience member, start by looking straight at that person and, if possible, addressing the person by name. Simply using the name often tends to lower the questioner's temperature somewhat, and it shows respect. If you show respect and that person doesn't show respect for you, everyone in the audience will know who is the good guy and who is the bad guy.

Then, as you answer, move your eyes toward another member of the audience and let that person ask the next question. This prevents your hostile questioner from getting in a follow-up question. It also allows you to spread your gaze around the room and doesn't turn your Q&A session into a one-on-one debate.

Another way to handle an aggressive questioner is to use that person's points as a gateway to another audience member or point you want to make. Years ago, I was president of a nonprofit board, and we had a lawyer member who wanted to dominate every conversation. Other board members complained to me about it (not that they needed to, he bothered me as well) and wanted a solution.

I didn't want to lose his services (or his contributions), but if I didn't take action, other members of the board were likely to walk away. I could not allow that to happen.

I eventually found a way to co-opt what he was saying and still get away from him. The next time he started into a long diatribe, I politely cut him off with "That's a good point. Let's pursue that and get some input from other board members on it." I would then turn to another member of the board and say, "Jim, why don't you pick up on that point, and then why don't you go into the budget issue that you had in mind." It worked; the conversation bully wasn't able to go back to his point because we had moved on, and everyone on the board got a chance to speak.

In a Q&A session, if you find yourself besieged by one person and the eye trick and satisfying and steering hasn't worked, try to include that person's point in your comments to someone else. Take the question, start to answer it, and then as you move to another person in the audience say, "Is [what that person asked] a big concern to you as well? If not, what is?" You are now taking a question from someone who is (hopefully) not going to be as aggressive.

What do you do if you open up the floor for questions but no one asks any? Besides whisper a prayer of thanksgiving, one option is to say, "Well, I know when I've spoken about this before people have asked . . ." and then throw in an easy question that you think might be on their minds. Often, this has the effect of "priming the pump," and other questions will follow. Plus, you've given yourself a chance to make your key points again.

Another option is to wrap-up by summarizing your talk. "Well, as I said . . ." and then giving your three key points. Then thank everyone and head off the stage.

Ending the Q&A

As a CEO, your time is precious. You don't have all day to spend fielding questions from everyone who has an opinion about what you've said. You've got decisions to make and other speeches to give. Also, the longer you take Q&A, the greater the likelihood that you will say something you'll regret. So how do you effectively end your Q&A session?

The first step is to set a time limit at the beginning. When you open it for questions, say, "I have time for a few questions," or "I've got about five minutes before I have to go, so if you have questions. . . ." This puts everyone on notice that you will not stand there all day.

Toward the end of your predetermined Q&A time, announce that you have time for one or two more questions. Then take those questions and, if it is appropriate, sum up by reiterating your key points. Thank everyone, accept your rapturous applause, and leave the podium.

Like everything else in this book, Q&A is a challenge, and it is also an opportunity. Successfully handling Q&A makes a CEO look more knowledgeable, approachable, open, and prepared. Not one of those is a bad thing. Don't view Q&A as a potential attack by evil forces; see it as a chance to let everyone know you are the right person to have in charge.

Tips

- Q&A preparation is an essential part of preparing your speech.
- Use the Q&A session to show your knowledge, handle difficult questions, and reaffirm or broaden your key points.
- Use your eyes to cue the person you want to ask a question and to get away from a hostile questioner.
- Go into greater depth about your key points in the Q&A session than you did in the speech.

CHAPTER 17

Speechwriter and Speaker: A Critical Alliance

"It usually takes more than three weeks to prepare a good impromptu speech."

—Mark Twain, American author

The relationship between speechwriter and speaker can be an uneasy alliance. It presents challenges for both, but it's an alliance that must be fruitful if the chief executive is to be presented at his best.

Perhaps no assignment is more challenging than writing for the President of the United States. While most chief executives can't devote a lot of face-to-face time to meetings with members of the speechwriting team, the chief executive of a large country probably has the least time of any of them. The writer must capture his voice, his personality, and his outlook on the world with little, if any, direct contact.

The stakes couldn't be higher. Whatever is said in a presidential speech is likely to go around the world and into the history books. That's why some of the world's smartest and best speechwriters end up on the White House writing staff.

Some go on to become legends in their own right, such as Ted Sorensen and Peggy Noonan. Sorensen wrote many of the memorable words uttered by John F. Kennedy, and Noonan penned many of those spoken by Ronald Reagan. Those were two of the greatest political speakers the Western world has ever known, but neither could have reached those heights without great material to deliver.

The same is true in business. There are no great executive speakers with poor writers, so the selection of an executive speechwriter and the development of the proper speaker-writer relationship must be a high priority for any company leader.

The problems are numerous and significant. The CEO is busy. His or her schedule is packed. The speechwriter stands much lower in corporate rank, a specialist good at his craft but not likely to command a whole lot of the boss's time and attention. Unlike a C-suite executive, the writer usually can't just pop into the corner office to get a question answered or an idea approved. This disparity in rank can cause the speechwriter to be hesitant to speak up with a question or suggestion, and the speechwriter may not even have the opportunity to do so. In some cases, the two rarely meet face-to-face. This puts a great burden on the speechwriter as he or she tries to capture the boss's voice and message.

When the executive rises to speak, it will be the speechwriter's words he utters, not his own. Everyone in that audience and beyond will interpret all that is said to be the executive's words and thoughts. It is not the speechwriter to whom the quotes will be attributed. Therefore, a close and constructive relationship between CEO and writer is essential.

Both are frustrated when the writer hands in the first draft of a speech and the speaker says, "That's not what I want to say at all."

Analyzing the Audience

There is a process that can result in a quicker and better meeting of the minds. It will take only 15 to 20 minutes initially and can avoid time wasted and frustration down the road.

Here is what I recommend.

Every talk of any kind, no matter by whom or for whom, should begin with an analysis of the audience. Without knowing the thoughts and interests of the audience it is impossible to form an effective strategy (i.e., the intended outcome of your speech). What do you want the audience to do, say, think, or feel? Not a word should be written until the strategy is clearly defined and agreed upon by the executive and the writer.

This is where your id does the talking. Sample objectives can be "I want to show I know this subject," "I want them to donate $50,000," "I want to get this legislation approved," or "I want my employees to work harder on this project."

Once you have determined your objective, every single thing you do in writing and delivering your speech is focused on achieving that objective.

Next, answer some basic questions about your audience. The purpose here is to help build the connection between you and them. Whenever one person addresses another group, there is an implied and often realistic divide between the speaker and audience. Knowing more about the audience and showing that knowledge in the talk helps you connect with them, which helps you to successfully deliver your messages and achieve your strategic objective.

The first question you need to ask is *Who are they?* How do they see themselves? For example, if you are speaking to a group of flight attendants, you should know that they see themselves as the "face" of the airline, as well as an important part of the safety team. You should let your writer know this, and he or she can choose whether to use that type of language in addressing the group.

Next, *Why are they there?* Are they volunteers or draftees? Your writer will use different language for people who chose to listen to you than he or she will for people who had no such choice.

What has recently happened for your audience, or *What is about to happen* that you should acknowledge? If they have achieved a goal or are about to celebrate an anniversary, you should say so. As I said before, this helps to bridge the gap and shows that you know and care about your audience.

What amuses them? Maybe even more important, *What offends them?* If you are speaking to a group of Yankees fans and you want to start with some humor, you could tell a joke at the expense of the Red Sox. However, do not make that same joke in Boston.

Next, *what connection* do you have to this group or members of the audience? If you know someone important in the audience, mention that you've spoken to him or her by name. "I had lunch with Jeff Waters the other day, and he told me that you are about to celebrate your 150th anniversary as a club. Congratulations." Or "Like you, I attended a small Midwestern university, so I know the challenges that can occur when people have never heard of your alma mater." Again, the idea is to show the audience that you are not that different from them, that you know them, and that you have an understanding of their issues and situation.

What is the expectation? What does the audience think you are going to discuss? What do they expect to get out of this presentation—information, marching orders, an apology? Make sure that you acknowledge this, if not meet it outright.

What are the adjacencies? Who is speaking before and after you, or what is coming up next or just finished when you get up to talk? Decide if you want to mention it. "I am proud to follow Bill Wennington on this dais, as I enjoyed seeing him play at St. John's and remember his seasons with the Bulls." Or "I know you've got a big dinner coming up as soon as I finish, and I don't want to keep you from it, but let me discuss for a few minutes why what we're doing is so important."

The question you're probably asking now is "How do I learn all of this?" By asking.

When you are asked to speak, find time to talk with someone from the group or someone who has a good knowledge of the audience. Typical questions can be "Is there anything coming up I should know about?" "What are they most proud of?" "What are they worried about?" "How do they see themselves?"

Once you have this information about your audience, you can start to work with your writer to craft an excellent talk.

Your Key Messages

Now that writer and speaker have a clear picture of the audience and a definition of what is sought from them, it's time to block out the key messages.

First, select the main theme—the headline you'd like to see in the newspaper, the bottom line on your story. Then pick three headline points, the same as the Must Air points we use for media interviews, that will make the case to the audience. Three. Not four, not five, not ten. Three.

Why three? Because the speaker can remember three, and so can everybody else. If you'll recall, we stated earlier that communication is not what the communicator knows or says but what the audience takes away. An audience can easily absorb a headline or theme line and three substantiating points.

Once the speaker and the writer have agreed on the three proof points, they should write those points down.

The next step is to select key examples and proofs that will support and expand on the points and write those down. In a few minutes, some very important work has been done.

The writer now has clear direction as to what the CEO wants and can work efficiently within that framework. We have eliminated the liklihood that the speaker will look at the writer's subsequent first draft and exclaim, "No, that's not what I had in mind at all." The basic framework is set.

Once the first draft is submitted, the two can go over it and come up with refinements and improvements to put it into final form.

This process saves time and frustration and therefore money. It allows smooth coordination in a limited timeframe, and there is less liklihood that the finished product will be disappointing to the speaker. The writer can return with a first draft that is likely to be mostly approved. Subsequent revisions can iron out any rough spots.

Sometimes a line or section will look good on paper but be clumsy or hard to deliver with the voice. To avoid this, the speaker should tell the writer to try reading the final draft out loud before submitting it. It's surprising how often writers find things that need to be revised or refined using this process.

So, now that we have a smooth, well-written speech, we're primed for success, right? Wrong.

Rehearsing the Talk

I can't tell you how many times speechwriters have told me, "I wrote this great speech for the boss, and he delivered it in such a way that all of the impact was lost." There is probably no greater frustration for a professional speechwriter than a good speech badly delivered.

No matter how experienced or skilled the speaker, rehearsal is an essential element of success for any speech. Many executives consider rehearsal to be reading the material over quietly late at night at home or in a hotel room. That is not rehearsal, and it is certainly not the best way to prepare for an important public appearance. Once again, let me state that things that read well to the eye don't always work well when spoken.

Any significant talk should be rehearsed in front of the speechwriter and the CEO's speech coach. If the CEO doesn't have a speech coach, one should be retained. People at the top don't speak publicly very often, so when they do, peak performance is called for. What they say and the way they say it may be remembered for a long time. A good coach can add a lot of polish to the delivery in a short time.

I recommend this rehearsal process: the speaker should first read through the entire text aloud, with no stopping. In addition to the obvious benefit of being able to time the talk, the writer and coach can hear the flow and rhythms of the work. They can make notes as they go as to what needs to be rewritten or what can be improved.

When the speaker comes across something clumsy or something he wants changed, he should simply say "mark," and the coach and speechwriter make a note of it. The writer and coach should also mark when they find something they would like altered. Then, upon review, copy changes can be made based upon what all three participants noted.

The next step is to do a video-recorded run-through, playing it back so the speaker can hear how he or she sounds and the coach can suggest improvements in delivery. That record-and-playback process should be repeated until the delivery reaches the desired level. It's best to do this in short segments, say two minutes at a time, refining the delivery of each portion before doing a final run-through of the entire talk. Yes, this process takes time, but it is a worthwhile investment for any major speech by a high-level official.

Finding the Right Writer

What I have said up to now is based on having a good speechwriter, but not every C-level executive has one. Some serious mistakes are often made in choosing the person for that role.

For one thing, speechwriting is a specialized craft. The fact that somebody can write a good report or a solid news release does not automatically make that person a speechwriter any more than a good novelist is the right person to prepare a required document for filing with the Securities and Exchange Commission.

How do you pick the right person for the job?

Writing skill is obviously important, but so is the ability to tell a story in an interesting and compelling way.

New York speechwriter Dana Rubin takes this view: "A speech is a vehicle for change. It should move an audience from one place to another. It takes you on a journey. The audience should not be the same when they walk out of a speech. They are going to be motivated to do something differently; they are going to be called to action." Not every writer can accomplish that.

Jeff Shesol, founding partner of West Wing Writers in Washington, D.C., and a former speechwriter for President Clinton, claims that "[a] speech is an argument for something. The most important thing, we often say around here [to fellow speechwriters] is 'You're not giving a speech; you're making an argument.' What is the fundamental thing that you've got to get up there and communicate? That needs to be the through line that runs from the start to the end of the speech."

It's important to find a speechwriter who can meet these standards.

What is not important for the writer is to come in with expertise in your field. That can be quickly learned. The ability to craft a first-rate speech is only developed over time.

Coca-Cola's Soltis lists these qualifications for a top-notch speechwriter:

- Personal compatibility with the speaker
- High energy, but calm under pressure
- Flexibility
- Deadline driven
- A thought leader, as opposed to a passive recorder
- The ability to capture the speaker's voice
- The ability to generate lots and lots of consistently good copy

Now you see why good speechwriters are prized in the halls of corporations.

Telling Stories

How do you measure the success level of a talk?

New York speechwriter Jim Holtje puts it this way: "The tell-tale sign of success usually is when you ask someone in the audience an hour after the speech 'What do you remember?' and they can pretty much go through what was said. What they will probably remember the longest, say a month or year later, are the stories. They are not likely to remember the statistics or numbers, but I can still quote stories in speeches that I heard years ago. That's a tell-tale sign that storytelling is extremely important."

I agree. If people remember the story long after, they probably also remember the point.

Holtje, who covers storytelling in detail in his 2011 book *The Power of Storytelling*, says, "Stories are how we make sense of the world and how we communicate that sense to others."[1]

He added, "Most of the time during a speech, people don't really start paying attention until the first story begins."

We can look to the long-running CBS television program *60 Minutes*, the most successful news feature program in the history of the medium, for a model. *60 Minutes* is known for its exposés, but every one of its features is skillfully told in story form. That storytelling is a key reason *60 Minutes* has been so successful, while a string of competing programs in the same genre have fallen short.

A good story can last for decades. Who can forget Hugh Heffner's tale that he left *Esquire* when they refused his request for a $5.00 raise? He then started *Playboy*, which soon outpaced his former publication and led to a multibillion-dollar empire.

What kind of stories work best? Stories that both engage and illustrate.

Says Holtje, "I've found that what people are most interested in are stories about CEOs before they got to the top. They especially like to hear about people overcoming adversity and succeeding despite the odds."

I find that good personal stories, modestly told, are the most effective ones. We look for such stories in our presentation training programs so that speechwriters can incorporate them into future texts.

It's often the speechwriter's job to ferret out good stories. "For an internal presentation," Holtje says, "the leader should talk about employees who have gone above and beyond the call of duty. For external speeches, the stories have to be chosen to present the speaker and the company as thought leaders. The stories must always align with the company's core business objectives."

What is the formula for a good speech? In Chapter 15, I mentioned that music, particularly vocal music, is a good model for the speaker. Rubin says it is also a good model for the speechwriter: "High notes and low notes, rhythm variations, unexpected cadenzas, all kinds of different elements to keep the audience surprised and engaged. The more we think of speeches as a performative piece, the more we can remember to add elements that entertain our audience and keep them engaged."

Breaking Some Rules

One thing I have stressed in this book is the importance of short sentences and short words in oral communication. However, as with any rule, there are exceptions. A speech that has only short sentences will lack the rhythm and variety that good speechwriters like Rubin stress. Variety in the length of sentences is also important to holding the attention of an audience.

An excerpt from John F. Kennedy's presidential inauguration speech on January 20, 1961, makes the point clearly:

> *Let every nation know, whether it wishes us well or ill, that we shall pay any price, bear any burden, meet any hardship, support any friend, oppose any foe, in order to assure the survival and the success of liberty.*
>
> *This much we pledge—and more.*
>
> *To those old allies whose cultural and spiritual origins we share, we pledge the loyalty of faithful friends. United, there is little we cannot do in a host of cooperative ventures. Divided, there is little we can do—for we dare not meet a powerful challenge at odds and split asunder.*

Try reading those words aloud. You will see that, while some of the sentences are long, the flow and phrasing are such that the material is easy for the speaker to deliver and for the listener to follow. It is superbly written (by Ted Sorensen) and was powerfully delivered by the young president.

There is an old axiom that reads "Rules are made to be broken." I agree, but only when there is a clear reason for it, such as changes in common usage. In one of the wonderful old Pogo comic strips, there is a line that I dearly love: "We have met the enemy, and it is us." Correct English usage would call for saying "it is we," but that just wouldn't work and wouldn't be the way most people would say it. It's also not the way those wonderful comic characters would say it.

The English language is always evolving, and many of the old rules are being cast aside. I once met a man on a train in Italy who held professorships at both The University of Bologna and UCLA. He contrasted English and Italian (he was quite fluent in both) and said that while he loved the beauty and charm of Italian, he enjoyed English more. The reason? "It's an organic language," he told me. "Italian is mostly fixed in place, while English is organic—constantly growing and changing. It's simply more interesting."

One of the most significant changes is the common usage of fragments rather than full sentences, both in spoken communication and in print. For example, a speaker may say, "Making this one change will do more for our industry. Much more. And do it right away."

Writing like that in English class would have immediately brought out the teacher's blue pencil, but such fragments can add power to a speech. Read that phrase aloud using the techniques outlined in Chapter 15 and see if you don't agree.

Another good technique that wouldn't be "allowed" in an essay is the use of questions, but essays are essays and speeches are speeches. Questions are a powerful tool for a speaker. They make an audience think, and they create a sense of dialogue between the speaker and the audience. They give a sense of two-way communication.

Here's an example of how questions can enhance a speech. First, I'll outline some points in the form of simple, declarative sentences:

> *Due to the high cost of materials, weather problems, an antiquated facility, and other considerations, we will be closing the Franklin-area plant next year. We will be moving our location to the Goldman area, into their new facility that was recently upgraded.*

Now let's cover the same material in the form of questions:

> *We have decided to close the Franklin area plant and move to the Goldman area. Why close Franklin? It's an old facility, we have had problems with the weather that has hurt business, and materials costs are higher there. Why Goldman? Its new facility, which was recently upgraded, and it offers a significant improvement in efficiency, materials, and cost.*

The latter has the audience thinking; the former may or may not have.

The Post-Mortem

Once a speech has been delivered, it's a good idea to do a brief postmortem between speechwriter and speaker whenever possible. What worked well and what didn't? What words, if any, were difficult or troublesome? What elements of this talk should be preserved for future use? How could this work have been improved upon?

The purpose here is not only to praise or critique both writer and speaker. It is to ensure that the next talk is even better written and delivered. By finding trouble spots, as well as areas that worked better than expected, both halves of this communication team can improve the output from the top level of the company.

Perhaps the hardest thing for any writer to do is write in someone else's voice. That is the challenge for the professional speechwriter, but it is a challenge that you, as the speaker, can mitigate through the steps I've outlined in this chapter. The potential reward is enormous: being seen as an erudite spokesperson for your organization and industry is priceless. Helping your speechwriter help you is time well spent.

Tips

- Meet with your speechwriter so he or she can learn your voice.
- Analyze your audience with him or her to ensure the best results.
- Practice your speeches with your speechwriter and speaking coach present.
- Running through the talk quietly in your hotel room is *not* rehearsal.
- Debrief after the talk.

Note

1. Holtje, Jim. *The Power of Storytelling: Captivate, Convince, or Convert Any Business Audience Using Stories from Top CEOs*, Prentice Hall, 2011.

CHAPTER 18

Humor: A Powerful Tool, but Handle with Care

"Once you get people laughing, they're listening and you can tell them almost anything."

—*Herbert Gardner, American author*

The stereotype of the CEO is of a humorless, overly serious, focused-only-on-the-bottom-line older white man (who is probably a little overweight) in a three-piece pinstriped suit, cigar in mouth, lackeys at his feet. As I'm sure you know by now, the stereotype is wrong. CEOs today come in all shapes, sizes, races, and personalities, not to mention both genders, but it is safe to say that "humorless" occurs more often than it should.

Humor, properly employed, contributes greatly to a person's success as a communicator. When misapplied, however, it can become an embarrassment or worse.

Leo Rosten once described humor as "the affectionate communication of insight."

Risks of Humor

Humor is often a commentary on the human condition—on our frustrations and foibles. However, it is a double-edged sword: it can offend as well as delight.

Humor is especially risky when speaking to people of a different cultural background. Until you really get to know another country's culture and sensitivities, it's best to leave your joke book at home. If you feel you have to be humorous, try all of your material on your local associates first. Be sure to tell them to laugh only when they are genuinely amused, not out of courtesy.

I recall news stories several years ago about a Japanese executive working in the United States. A friendly man, he tried to use humor in his staff meetings, but because of cultural differences, his audience was never sure when he was joking. As a result, they rarely laughed. So he came up with a couple of small signs, one saying "Joke" and the other reading "Serious." He would hold up the appropriate one so people would laugh or not laugh on cue. As I recall, his sign technique produced more humor than what he said.

The safest kind of humor is directed at one's own shortcomings in matters of relative inconsequence. A CEO might properly make a joke about his ineptitude at golf but would be ill-advised to deliver one about his management skills or the quality of his company's products, or worse, at the expense of his management team.

One of the most important elements of humor is a level of safety in the audience. The listener or reader must know that there is no real damage coming from the words being said or actions being shown. Moe hitting Curly with a board is funny in a Three Stooges short (if you find it such); your actually hitting someone with one is not. The audience for a movie knows that the actors were not seriously injured in the action; thus they are free to laugh.

The same has to be true with any joke or humor coming out of a leader. You cannot, *cannot* make jokes about things you have control over that could adversely affect your audience. The most obvious example is joking about firing people. While you might find it hilarious, the people whose jobs depend on you will not find it as such (well, some might, but for a larger group it's a dangerous area to tread). CEOs cannot joke about closing factories, shipping jobs overseas, discontinuing product lines, or the physical safety of employees or customers.

Despite these warnings and caveats, humor has great value to a corporate leader. Why? It relaxes audiences and helps them build a bond with the speaker. Self-effacing humor in particular makes a CEO more likable, and likability is directly related to credibility and trust. We put more faith in people we like.

Connecting Humor to Your Points

One of the most critical things to remember when using humor in a presentation is that it must relate to the topic of your talk. Too many times I've seen a speaker start with a funny story, then move on to the body of the speech without any connection to the story. The result is an audience that remembers a funny duck joke but not the points of the speech.

One of the most important sentences in any speech is the one that connects the icebreaker (whether it's a joke, anecdote, statistic, graphic, something else) to the body of the talk. If you start a speech with a duck joke, the first sentence after the punch line has to show how that story relates to the situation the speaker, the audience, or both are in. Tell the audience that you are the duck, or they are the hunter, or the line that the hunter said is particularly apt considering current proposed regulations. The joke, like all of your other speech enhancements, is there to reinforce your key points, not overshadow them. (You can read much more about this in Chapter 15.)

The Humorous Style

Using humor, especially for the first time, requires sticking one's neck out. It often involves playing a role or catching a voice. It demands timing, the right phrases, and pauses. Most of all, it requires practice beforehand to get it just right.

Numerous American presidents have used humor to great effect, but none more so than Ronald Reagan. He was the master of the short story and the quip.

Here's a classic from a speech he gave to the Republican National Convention in 1992:

> *Tonight is a very special night for me. Of course, at my age, every night's a very special night. After all, I was born in 1911. Indeed, according to the experts, I have exceeded my life expectancy by quite a few years. Now this is a source of great annoyance to some, especially those in the Democratic Party.*[1]

It was wry, clever, and self-effacing. No doubt the audience loved it.

One thing that made Reagan so successful in delivering humor was that he obviously savored it himself. When he started to tell a funny story, his face would light up and his body and his delivery became animated. He made it clear that what was to follow was going to be funny, that he enjoyed it, and the audience should also.

Business leaders can learn a lot from this master of humor. Not everybody can be as good in employing humor as Reagan or other presidential masters such as Obama and Kennedy, but anyone can deliver humor at an acceptable level.

Humor should be personal and human—something anyone in an audience can relate to. It is often a slight exaggeration of reality but has truth at its core.

Humor can stem from stories, commentary, or quotes. There are a number of online sources of quotes. It can take time to find the right one, but I think it's worth the effort.

Sometimes you can steal a gag from a comedian and turn it into a useful vehicle for where you're speaking. I've always enjoyed a line by George Gobel, whose network comedy show in the late 1950s was one of the funniest programs on television. He once quipped, "My father was the town drunk! And we lived in Chicago!"

I've used that as an opener in Chicago, followed quickly by "I see Chicago has changed a bit since then." People enjoy the story, nobody gets offended, and it gets a laugh because it brings back memories of how "wet" Chicago was during Prohibition.

Telling the Joke

Great material alone does not make for successful humor. It has to be properly delivered.

There is a very old joke (and one that many speakers have used) about a new prisoner's first night in his cell. In the middle of the night someone in the cell block yelled out, "Fourteen!" and all the other prisoners laughed. A minute later another yelled, "Seven!" and the prisoners laughed again. The new inmate asked his cellmate what was going on. "Well," he replied, "most of have been here for so long that we've been telling the same jokes for decades. So we numbered all of the jokes we tell, and now we just call out the number and we all know the joke." The new inmate asked if he could try it. His cellmate replied, "Sure," and after a beat the newbie cried out, "Four!" He was met with total silence. He asked his cellmate what went wrong. His cellmate replied, "Hey, some people can tell a joke; some people can't."

I've often had executives tell me, "I delivered something funny in what I thought was the right style but nobody laughed. Why?"

There could be several reasons, but if the story, comment, or quote is funny and appropriate to this particular audience, the problem has to be in the delivery. With proper coaching and practice, that is fixable.

The most common reason for a joke bombing is that it was told in a timid manner, perhaps apologetically and without conviction. I mentioned earlier that success requires sticking your neck out. That means delivering your joke as if you know it is funny. If you believe it is, deliver it with the strength of your convictions. If it isn't funny, don't use it.

Another common problem is that speakers sometimes don't let the audience realize that they are hearing a joke. For the most part, deadpan or dry delivery of humor at the beginning of a speech doesn't work. Your delivery doesn't need to be as manic as 1970s Steve Martin, but 1980s Steven Wright isn't going to work, either. A good smile, using voices or inflection as mentioned earlier, and a solid pause before and after the punch line should alert the audience that they should expect "the funny."

If a joke doesn't work, here are some of the most likely reasons:

- The speaker didn't send a cue that the moment was meant to be humorous.
- There was no pause after the punch line to let the laugh come.
- It was the wrong material for that particular audience.
- Sometimes, people are smiling or laughing inside and just don't feel comfortable laughing out loud in that particular environment.

What should you do if a laugh line flops? Just smile and go on with your talk. Making a reference to it will likely just embarrass you and them.

Humor is *not* for everyone. As the prison joke says, not everyone can tell a joke. Practice helps, but there are some people who just cannot sell a story to save their proverbial lives. If you are one of those people, don't try to be funny. It will hurt your reputation (and your audience). Everyone should try to use humor and practice it to get comfortable with it, but if you have given it a fair shot over a long-enough period of time and you find that your stories just fall flat, then it's time to stick to other ways of getting an audience's attention. As W. C. Fields said, "If at first you don't succeed, give up. Nobody makes a monkey out of me twice."

Properly employed, humor can be a great aid to communication, especially as an icebreaker and to illustrate key points. But it has to be used carefully and wisely.

Tips

- Have the courage to insert humor into your talks.
- Don't use anything that isn't funny to you.
- Make sure your humor is appropriate to the audience and situation.
- Give audiences cues as to when to laugh.
- Try to stay away from excessively familiar material.
- Don't get discouraged if they don't laugh every time you think they should.

Note

1. http://odur.let.rug.nl/~usa/P/rr40/speeches/rnc92.htm

PART V

The World Outside

CHAPTER 19

The Role of Philanthropy: Doing Well by Doing Good

"Non-profit activity is essential to a corporation."
—Stephen K. Orr, consultant

Philadelphia merchant and advertising pioneer John Wanamaker once said, "I know that half the money I spend on advertising is wasted; but I can never find out which half."

Many CEOs, especially those new to the job, raise that and similar questions about the time and money their companies spend on philanthropies. Is it wasted? Does it really do any good? Is it a good use of the organization's resources? Are they the right causes? Does it add anything to the bottom line?

Like advertising, direct benefits from philanthropic organizations are hard to quantify. Perhaps it's enough to say that, like advertising, some of the companies that devote the most resources to philanthropy are also some of the most successful.

Benefits of Philanthropy

Stephen K. Orr, managing partner and co-founder of Orr Associates, Inc. (OSI), told me such activity pays off in a variety of ways. Orr's Washington, D.C.- and New York City-based firm is a leader in consulting to nonprofit organizations.

Not only is there great value to a CEO being on a nonprofit board, Orr says, "It must be viewed as a part of his or her responsibility in running the company."

"The profit and nonprofit worlds have come together considerably in the last 20 years," he told me. "Executives are realizing the importance of nonprofit activities to their companies."

But just what are the benefits? One is an improved image of the company and its leaders. You may remember the example in Chapter 2 about how the creation of the Bill and Melinda Gates Foundation helped humanize the image of both the founder of Microsoft and the company, both of whom had often been described as ruthless in their business practices.

As I will point out in Chapter 21, the response of the news media, the public, and the blogosphere in a crisis will be heavily influenced by the perception of a company and its leaders going in. So, a good image achieved through corporate generosity or other means is clearly an asset in hard times.

Another benefit is the contacts that are made. Sitting on a major board means getting to know some of your peers in other firms, and you never know when that can lead to business.

External and Internal Benefits

Sixty CEOs of Fortune 500 companies, meeting in New York in February 2012 under the auspices of the Committee Encouraging Corporate Philanthropy, agreed that today's consumers hold companies accountable for engaging in behaviors that reinforce the well-being of society. Sixty-nine percent felt their companies' engagement efforts were rewarded by consumers but conceded they were unable to measure it; the jury is still out regarding the impact on the bottom line.

Some of the benefits of involvement in nonprofits generally go unseen. Orr says nonprofits are a great leadership training ground for the young executive. He put it this way: "Service in nonprofits is important to the ascent of any executive. It helps people understand the culture of the company. It is essential to moving into the CEO chair."

Here is a point that surprised me. Orr said, "People stay with a company longer if they are involved in nonprofit work that they like. It validates their passion, reducing turnover."

I thought about that for a minute and concluded he was right. I have owned my own business since 1990. As a result, I've been able to choose what organizations to support and on what boards to serve. If I worked for someone else and leaving would mean giving up those board positions of organizations I deeply believe in, I would think twice. It certainly would be a consideration in deciding whether to change jobs.

One of the organizations that Orr leads is called Youth, I.N.C. It's an umbrella group that helps organizations that serve young people in New York City in many ways, including improving fund-raising practices, building boards, and funding critical elements of infrastructure.

Its record is impressive. During its first 18 years, Youth, I.N.C. raised $40 million, empowered 100 youth nonprofit programs, affected the lives of 600,000 New York City children and youth, placed more than 120 corporate professionals as nonprofit board members, trained over 600 corporate executives as potential board members, and awarded over $1.3 million in capacity-building grants.

The board of Youth, I.N.C. reads like a who's-who of Wall Street. Are these savvy men and women, whose time is so valuable, telling us something about the value of corporate participation in worthwhile causes?

Finding Your Philanthropy Partner

How do you choose the right causes? Michael E. Porter and Mark R. Kramer, writing in the *Harvard Business Review*, have contended that most companies don't get it right, saying the majority of corporate contribution programs are diffuse and unfocused.[1]

Most CEOs have a cause that is close to their hearts. While it is tempting to throw the company's weight behind that issue, care must be taken to make sure that such work would be in the company's best interest.

Almost any expert will tell you that philanthropic activity should align with corporate objectives. It should also reinforce the corporate identity and message.

Avon, the global cosmetics company that bills itself as "The Company for Women," went to the source in establishing the Avon Foundation. CEO Andrea Jung told me, "We went out to women in markets all over the world, to our constituents, our sellers, as well as our consumers, to ask them what issues that affected women would they be most interested in seeing the company support. And the answers came back. The first was obviously women's health, and one of the leading issues in women's health is breast cancer." So that became a prime cause for Avon.

She continued. "A second very important cause that came up, again, grassroots from all the countries in the world, was the issue of domestic violence or violence against women. I mean, it's alarming, but there are one out of three women affected by some version of violence against women, which is a daunting statistic. And it crosses geographies, it crosses incomes, and it is a major issue, so we felt that we should take this issue on. We did so in 2004, so we have a second very, very important cause."

One thing you may notice about all the charities I've mentioned in this chapter is that they are not political in nature. The best charities for any corporation to be involved in are those which almost no one could disagree with. Who would argue in favor of breast cancer, violence against women, or not improving the lives of New York City's underprivileged children?

However, aligning with a political party or movement can backfire, as many customers might strongly disagree with the goals and ideals of the group. To paraphrase a familiar trope, use the KISS method—Keep It Safe, Stupid.

How Philanthropy Helps Your Corporate Image

Charitable giving is, unfortunately, on the wane. The Chronicle of Corporate Philanthropy reports that 71 percent of foundations said their contributions would drop or remain flat this year, following a 3.5 percent decline last year. Especially hard hit are local organizations because the globalization of business has caused leaders to think less about the home front.

But one company that thinks locally is Time Warner Cable. CEO Glenn Britt says local participation is important, noting, "[w]hile we're a pretty big company, in your community we're a local company. What we do for the community, if we do it right, is appreciated by the people who live there, so hopefully they'll be more likely to buy our service. It's certainly appreciated by the employees who live there."

Britt has brought up another advantage to local corporate generosity: employee pride and morale. That is a factor that certainly should not be overlooked in making funding decisions.

Britt says, "I spend a fair amount of time working in and around what we've decided is our main philanthropic effort, the so-called STEM education—Science, Technology, Engineering, and Math. So I actually appear publicly on that subject. I'm on a presidential task force on STEM that President Obama created. It's a good thing to do. But, in a more 'dollars and cents' way, I'm doing it because it's really in our business interest to do so."

Think of the message that his being on a presidential task force sends to employees, shareholders, and an industry. It's big. Very big. This man matters and so does his company.

Still another factor for the cable company is the impression such activity makes on local leaders. Cable is a regulated industry, and what local government officials and community leaders think about a cable company is important.

Smart companies not only align their giving and executive participation with their corporate objectives but they also tap into the major issues of the day. Perhaps no company has done more to burnish its image through good works than Starbucks. Part of the secret of its success is tying into key issues, such as its highly touted fair-trade practices for coffee growers.

The biggest concern in the United States today is the economy and jobs, so Starbucks is raising money through the new Create Jobs for USA Fund, providing funding and heavy promotion for the effort. It's a good policy and good public relations.

Cisco seemed to find the perfect combination of self-interest and public good a few years ago when it created the Cisco Networking Academy to train computer network administrators. It addressed a need for workers in its operation, while providing attractive job opportunities to high school graduates.

Companies engage in philanthropic activities for a wide variety of reasons. Some do it just for publicity and an improved public image, but handle with care: you can easily be seen as doing things only for your image.

In a *Harvard Business Review* article, Porter and Kramer tell of a large tobacco company that spent $75 million on charitable organizations in 1999 and then launched a $100 million advertising campaign to publicize them.[2] That's a story you don't want to see on the front page of *The New York Times*.

Because the company, Philip Morris, reportedly spent more money telling the world about its act than on the act itself, it is easy to conclude that corporate image was the primary and perhaps only motivation. This undoes some, if not all, of the good will gained from the program.

Corporate philanthropy is pretty much expected from any company of any size. The exact nature and extent of it is an important decision. Using the tips I've outlined here, your charitable work should reap benefits not only for the not-for-profit you align with, but for your company and your own image. So long as you are not seen as doing it for the "wrong" reasons, your program should help everyone involved.

Tips

- Consider philanthropy a key component of your corporate image and activities.
- Find charities that make sense for your company and your customer base.
- Consider current events and personal interests when looking for a good cause.
- Don't spend more on publicizing your works than you contributed to them.

Notes

1. Porter, Michael E. and Mark R. Kramer. "The Competitive Advantage of Corporate Philanthropy," *Harvard Business Review*, December 2002.
2. Ibid.

CHAPTER 20

Advocating for Your Company

"The greatest ability in business is to get along with others and to influence their actions."

—John Hancock, American independence leader

The majority of a CEO's communication with the public comes through media interviews, speeches, and investor relations activities. There are times, however, when he or she must get more directly involved in a situation. When public events or proposed changes in rules or laws are going to affect the company, or when the company wants to clearly position itself on a current issue, the CEO may need to get out in front personally.

There are several venues for this type of action, but let me name two, one obvious, the other perhaps less so: trade associations and professional societies. Circumstances will dictate which one to use, but both can have value in getting a desired resolution or staking out a position.

Working with Trade Associations

I can think of no sizable businesses that aren't involved in one or more trade organizations. For most, it's a necessity. With frequent threats from proposed legislation and regulation, and sometimes a need to get old laws and regulations changed, someone has to be protecting the industry's back (and thus the company's) in national and state capitals.

One of the biggest advantages of working through a trade association is the power of numbers. Glenn Britt, CEO of Time Warner Cable and a former president and current board member of the National Cable and Telecommunications Association (NCTA), says, "Perceptions are everything. If you take an individual cable company, people tend to underestimate how large we are. So, working together, we're able to have a lot more clout in places like Washington." Britt has been a highly visible and outspoken advocate on a number of issues affecting his industry.

In addition, the board of directors of NCTA reads like a who's-who of the heads of the top companies in the industry. I have no doubt that this high-level executive visibility and activism has been a factor in the cable industry's successes in Washington over the years.

The trade association's influence cannot be overestimated. Its speaking as one voice demonstrates not only the power of its members but also underlines the seriousness of the issue. If one company, say a restaurant operator, complains about a proposed law or regulation, it may get some attention, but if the National Restaurant Association raises the same complaint, it will get more public support and more government response.

Benefits of Professional Groups

Opportunity to lead change or establish a position sometimes comes from unexpected places. While many CEOs see an advantage to connecting with trade organizations, fewer feel that way about professional societies, in which the individual, not the company, is the member. But William Murray, chief operating officer and de facto head of the 20,000-member Public Relations Society of America (PRSA), says such an outlook may be leaving opportunity on the table. He contends that professional groups can provide an effective platform for a company to make a statement about its values and lead an important industry discussion.

"Right now," he said, "PRSA is addressing an issue that everybody in the profession cares about: ethics. Participation in this dialogue is an opportunity for a public relations company CEO to position himself or herself in terms of leadership and business acumen on a critical issue and portray the agency as one that values and practices good ethics."

During my tenure as chair of PRSA's international section in the early 2000s, we decided to tackle a key issue of the day: why the United States had such difficulty communicating with the rest of the world. We scheduled annual symposia at such places as the National Press Center in Washington, D.C., and United Nations headquarters in New York. While the serious and specific nature of the event assured that it would not draw large crowds, the impact of the program was significant.

We attracted some powerful speakers, including Washington influentials, think-tank leaders, and CEOs of some of the major public relations firms. The CEOs wanted to make a statement: that their firms were global in thought and action, and they themselves were thought leaders whose insights and capabilities could help their client companies, and perhaps nations, position themselves better. It also said something that they presented in the same forums as people such as the head of the Council on Foreign Relations and the vice-chairman of the 9/11 Commission.

Leaders of companies, and those who wish to be leaders, should not overlook the benefits of participation in professional or industry organizations.

Direct CEO Involvement

The job of reaching out to governments usually falls to industry lobbyists and the company's own government relations team, but there are times when a CEO needs to be personally involved and in the spotlight. Think, for example, of the U.S. government's bailouts of the auto and financial services industries. They could not have been accomplished without the CEOs of the firms most affected personally taking their arguments to Washington.

Another good example of when a chief executive can be more effective than a trade association comes from Murray. He cites two instances from his earlier tenure in the number two position at the Motion Picture Association of America (MPAA).

Tax policies are a critical issue for the movie industry. Sometimes it takes the involvement of a CEO to get a policy change that will enable a movie to be shot on location in a city like New York or Chicago rather than the studio trying to create a New York or Chicago look on a back lot in Hollywood. When a company can make the economics of filming in such cities work, everybody wins. The movie company has a film with more realism and wider scenic possibilities, and the cities' economies are bolstered.

Murray says a studio CEO can sometimes fly in and make the case for a tax rebate or other considerations by pointing to the economic benefits to the city and by suggesting that a successful movie shoot could lead to three or four more being filmed in the same city. That's a job MPAA could not do or, at least, not do as well.

The same is true on a national level when hearings are being conducted on an issue that could hurt an industry, says Murray. "Bob Iger, the CEO of Disney, can speak in a way that a trade association can't in regard to how a change in a copyright law could affect jobs, investments, and shareholders."

Your Advocacy Messages

Whether the emissary is a corporate leader or the head of a trade organization, positions need to be well crafted and tailored to diverse audiences.

A good study in successfully defining an issue comes from Kathleen Jaeger, who headed the Generic Pharmaceutical Association from 2002 to 2010. During the last two decades, there have been some epic battles in Washington between the branded pharmaceutical companies and those that manufacture generic drugs. The pharmaceutical companies tried a variety of tactics to block or slow the introduction of generics, frequently raising questions about the safety and effectiveness of generic drugs.

"But when you filtered it all down," she told me, "it wasn't about safety; it was all about market share. These companies wanted to protect product monopolies."

The generics industry had to find a theme line that would register with a wide variety of audiences. Those audiences included employers, unions, government officials, thought leaders, and a host of others.

The line chosen was simple and effective: "consumer access to affordable medicine." You can see how that would play across a broad spectrum.

Once the theme line was chosen, it had to be backed up. "We were able to use a lot of the tenets from our media training with a lot of stakeholders and applications—Congressional hearings, talking to consumer groups, think tanks, policy makers, union leaders, and even corporate boards."

That meant having the same theme line and catch phrases for all audiences but tailoring the Must Air points and examples to the particular audience. "We would always have our sound bites in our pockets before we walked out the door," she said.

The association's efforts were successful. Today nearly 69 percent of prescriptions are filled with generic medicines, and the industry has grown from $1 billion in annual revenues in the United States to $63 billion.

When facing challenging public issues, companies sometimes have a tendency to leave it up to legal, or lobbying. While each of these can be effective, the CEO and the industry trade association will have a greater impact. No one disputes that advocacy is essential to business success. The question is who advocates, when, and in what venue(s). For each company, that's a CEO decision.

Tips

- Consider advocacy for the company's positions as part of the CEO's job.
- Be ready to speak for the industry, when appropriate, on key issues.
- Consider both trade associations and professional societies as vehicles for achieving change and emphasizing your company's values.
- Craft your messages carefully with a common theme, but vary the details and examples to fit the group you are addressing.

PART VI

It's Crunch Time

CHAPTER 21

Crisis: A CEO's Supreme Test

"Next week there can't be any crisis. My schedule is already full."
—Henry Kissinger, former U.S. Secretary of State

Thousands of books, articles, and manuals have been written about crisis handling and prevention in recent years, but apparently too few CEOs have read them.

Virtually anyone who follows the news can tick off a long list of incidents in which organizations were caught unprepared and bungled their way into bad outcomes. The early 2010s have already given us Goldman Sachs, Tokyo Electric, BP, Toyota, and Susan G. Komen for the Cure, among many others.

Are more crises occurring now than in the past? That's hard to say, but there is clearly more media coverage of crises these days and thus more chances for companies to help or hurt their image through crisis handling.

Crises can't always be avoided, but the damage can almost always be mitigated.

The key question about a crisis occurring in an organization of any size is not "whether"; it's "when" "how bad," and "is everything in place for a quick and effective response"?

Management guru Peter Drucker once said the one predictable thing in any organization is crisis. He noted, "The most important thing is to anticipate crisis. Not to avert it, but to anticipate it. To wait until the crisis hits is already abdication. You cannot prevent a major crisis, but you can build an organization that is battle-ready."

As one crisis specialist put it, "[w]hen you hear the thunder, it's a little late to start building the ark."

CEOs should expect to face at least one crisis of significance during their tenure, and perhaps more. How many and how bad depends more on how the company is managed than on fate.

Two things are revealed about a company during a crisis: its culture, and its level of preparation. People will learn quickly what a company values when tough times hit. Does it reward open communication and transparency, or does it reward covering up? Has it worked in advance to anticipate and mitigate difficult situations? Is the leadership responsive, on top of things, and competent to handle it?

In a crisis, the public will very quickly decide if a company is run by good people who had something bad happen to them or by bad people who caused something bad to happen. Are you the "fireman" or the "arsonist"?

While the nature of the crisis is important, the fact is the handling of the crisis almost always has a greater impact on the company's reputation than the crisis itself. It sometimes doesn't seem to matter how serious the incident is as long as it is handled well. Conversely, a small problem handled terribly could do long-term damage to a company's reputation.

Much as too few CEOs read books on crises, too few pay attention to history, especially the history of things that happen in their own industry.

Similar Incidents, Different Responses, Different Results

Two oil incidents in the 1980s offer a sharp contrast in how a crisis is handled and the effect on reputation. The 1989 spill from the Exxon Valdez led to a botched response that hurts the company's reputation to this day (23 years later as of this writing). The company appeared to stall on its response, seemed slow to clean up the spill, tried to dodge responsibility for the accident when it initially claimed the captain was drunk, and stonewalled reporters covering the story. Exxon became a symbol of bungled crisis response.

A smaller but no less important incident occurred in 1988 involving the Ashland Oil Company in Pittsburgh, Pennsylvania. One of the company's fuel tanks collapsed, sending oil down the Monongahela and Ohio Rivers and polluting the drinking water of thousands of residents in Pennsylvania and neighboring states. Thousands of people were lining up to get their drinking water from tank trucks for several days. However, the company was upfront, apologized, took responsibility, explained questionable decisions that may have led to the spill, and worked feverishly on the cleanup. The company's reputation was held level (or even improved) as a result of its response to their crisis. The company was widely praised for its positive response to the incident.

Crisis handling clearly affects a company's bottom line. An Oxford University study in the 1990s delved extensively into the financial impact of good and bad crisis handling. It found that companies that were perceived to have handled a crisis poorly saw their stock drop 15 percent compared to the overall market 50 weeks after the crisis hit. However, companies that were considered to have handled their crises well saw their stock rebound to market level around 5 weeks later, and after 50 weeks were, on average, 7 percent above market value. That's a 22 percent difference. Not only does mishandling a crisis reduce a company's value, but handling it well actually increases its reputation and value. The difference can be quite substantial.

Types of Crises

Perhaps the first question to ask is "What is a crisis?" I define it as any unexpected occurrence that:

- Threatens injury to the general public, customers, and/or employees
- Disrupts a community's lifestyle or threatens its safety
- Calls the policies or actions of the company or organization into question
- Threatens the short- or long-term reputation of the company or organization
- Interferes with the ability of the company or organization to operate normally

Crises come in many types and sizes. There is the sudden and unavoidable, such as a hurricane or earthquake. Another is the simmering one where management fails to address a problem that has the potential to turn into a full-blown crisis. There is also the self-inflicted incident, often the result of a bad policy decision that has unanticipated consequences.

Let's look at examples of failures in each of these areas:

- **Unavoidable: Tokyo Electric and Power.** The March 2011 earthquake and tsunami were unavoidable, but TEPCO's preparation for a disaster was woefully inadequate, and the company communicated so badly afterward that the government took over the communication role. The events of nature were unavoidable, but the PR bungling was not.
- **Simmering: News Corporation.** The international media empire headed by Rupert Murdoch encouraged, or at least condoned, illegal and unethical acts by reporters and its British tabloid newspapers, including phone hacking of government officials, celebrities, and crime victims. The revelations resulted in an international scandal and the shuttering of the highly profitable *News of the World*. Numerous investigations and several indictments have ensued, along with massive negative news coverage.
- **Self-inflicted: Susan G. Komen for the Cure.** The not-for-profit stirred outrage when it cut off its funding for breast cancer screening

by Planned Parenthood, apparently caving in to political pressure by anti-abortion groups. Then Komen's leaders tried to assume the role of victim when a social media firestorm erupted and contributors started closing their pocketbooks. Claiming that you are the victim of unfair and unwarranted attacks only worsens the situation.

Why are so many companies unprepared when a crisis hits? There are many reasons, but the most common are:

- **"It can't happen here."** Too many companies and organizations put their heads in the sand or just hope beyond hope. Many are afraid (figuratively or literally) to thoroughly examine their operations to see what could go wrong, how it could go wrong, and what the damage could be. Also, they may have too much confidence in the response capabilities of their employees. It doesn't matter how stringent your hiring policies are; it is still possible that someone who is not perfect at his or her job is going to be hired. No matter where you recruit, you are not going to get a superhuman. People are people, and sometimes they will not act as you want when a problem occurs. Successful CEOs look at their operations, determine where things could go wrong, and have plans in place to handle problems when and if they occur.
- **Not having a crisis plan or having one that is out of date.** Crisis plans are something that too many people "plan to get to." However, it is critical that every organization or company big enough to have a CEO have such a plan. Every key employee should have a copy of the plan, have a source of online access to it, and should know what his or her responsibilities are if a crisis hits.
- **Cutbacks.** All too often, the person who is responsible to make sure the company is adequately prepared for disaster has been let go, and no one is given that responsibility after he or she leaves. In a good crisis plan the responsibilities are delineated by job title, not by individual. For example, in the plan it should say that communication with the police will be handled by the head of security, not "Bob will call the police." This ensures that when Bob leaves, the next head of security knows that this is part of his job in a crisis.
- **No clear crisis organizational structure.** The wrong people call the shots, or everybody calls his own shots. In a crisis, it is vital that only the right people are making the key decisions. The naming of those people must be done in advance and is a critical part of any crisis plan.
- **People fail to gauge the full impact on various constituencies.** All too often, a company or organization doesn't take into account the effect its actions might have on people or the environment. While sometimes this is due to hubris (who cares about anything outside these doors?),

more often it's simply due to not taking the time and effort to determine how the company's actions and policies could affect the rest of the world. This is one of the PR executive's most important functions: letting upper management know the organization's image in the "real world" and how its actions or inactions could affect that image.

Crisis Preparation

The key to crisis handling, as in all other communication, is preparation. There are steps that every company and organization needs to take now to be ready before a crisis hits.

Every company must have a crisis response plan. Most major corporations have one today or have created one at some point. However, as was mentioned before, I often find they are out of date. It's surprising, for example, that some plans don't include how to use social media in a crisis. As we saw in the Arab Spring, social media is a powerful global force that will drive events. Many also don't have the most current information about internal or external contacts—who's in what position, their phone or email, and so on. Many times plans aren't updated after mergers, acquisitions, or selling off units. The crisis plan should be revisited often, especially after any major change to the organization.

The first step in creating a plan is to identify the crisis situations most likely to hit the organization. The CEO, or someone designated by the CEO, should ask leaders of key units what is the worst thing that could happen in terms of causing deaths, injuries, loss of public confidence, or financial damage to the company. The chief executive must get these leaders to be frank; claiming that "nothing could go wrong" or that "we have systems in place to handle everything" does a disservice to the company and is setting it up for failure.

The next step is to examine the organization's state of readiness. Is there a crisis plan? Is it comprehensive and up to date? Is it readily accessible online for those who may need it? Do employees know how to access it? Is there a functioning crisis team? Do they meet regularly to discuss potential crises and how they will handle them? Are new members of the team brought up to date when they join?

It's important to identify people likely to be in the spotlight and to be sure they get the training they will need to handle an emergency. Media training is a must, as is some real media experience for those likely to be interviewed. This will reduce the chance that they will freeze up on camera or say what they shouldn't say. They also have to be kept up to date on company policies and situations so they don't need to have a quick "read up" when a crisis hits.

Crisis simulations should be conducted in which executives, including the CEO, are confronted with a realistic, developing scenario and required to come up with a quick response plan. The exercise should be pressure-packed, with the participants having to constantly react to changing circumstances. This not only helps prepare your executives for the real thing, but it also works as a team-building exercise. In addition, it often reveals which executives respond best under pressure. A two-day session is recommended for the first time the group is trained, with perhaps shorter refreshers down the road.

My firm once conducted a crisis readiness program for a utility company that operated a number of nuclear power plants. Their people performed superbly during the exercises—they were trained on a regular basis—but the company learned something that was important and previously unknown: local officials were not up to speed on how to handle a nuclear accident or an evacuation of any kind. Consequently, the utility company retained Virgil Scudder & Associates to put together a special program for these local government officials. This was an outstanding example of corporate responsibility and rule number one in crisis management: look ahead at what could happen and evaluate the level of preparation for it.

Sometimes role-playing gets too close to home. My firm once conducted a crisis readiness program for shopping center managers that used a scenario in which two gangs carry a dispute into a mall and get into a heated exchange that turns into a fatal shooting. Not long afterward, that very thing happened at a mall run by one of the managers in the training. There was only one significant difference between rehearsal and reality: our scenario had three people dead, but fortunately, in the real-world event, only one died. The manager later described the training experience as "invaluable" in dealing with the real situation.

Another important part of crisis preparation is to have good relationships with outside organizations you might need in a crisis. If you are in a regulated industry, it's a good idea for someone on your crisis team to have a good working relationship with someone in authority at the government agency. For example, if you work in the nuclear field, it's useful for your head of operations to know someone at the Nuclear Regulatory Commission and state regulatory agencies. This lessens the chances that the government agencies will come out strongly against you if you run into problems. It doesn't guarantee that you won't feel some heat from them, but it makes public criticism less likely. The CEO's job here is get assurance that the proper contacts are in place.

It's also important to have a positive image in the general public before disaster strikes. A company that flies under the radar, avoiding media coverage and involvement in the community, is at a distinct disadvantage when a crisis hits. A known and respected company will get better treatment from the media and be better able to convince the public that it does the right thing.

I've often told clients, "You don't want the first time people hear of you to be when the fire trucks are pulling up to your factory." A strong Corporate Social Responsibility (CSR) program can create goodwill for you before, during, and after a crisis.

So now you are ready for when disaster strikes. Now let's look at the steps you need to take when your crisis goes live.

What to Do When Crisis Hits

The first step is to determine whether or not the situation really is a crisis. Too many times a company has escalated a "problem" to a "crisis" by overreacting to the initial situation. The most frequent way this happens is by having the CEO or other high official respond to something that doesn't rise up to his or her level. A problem that the CEO discusses can be automatically raised to the perceptual level of crisis by such involvement.

Using the criteria at the beginning of the "Types of Crises" section of this chapter, ask if the situation threatens anyone's health or well-being, the company's reputation or its ability to do business. If the answer is yes to any of these, then activate your crisis plan. It is amazing and frustrating how many companies go through all the steps of crisis preparedness and then fail to take the appropriate steps when one hits.

I remember an incident in Hawaii that raised some of these questions. One of our client's ships had accidentally spilled some oil off the coast of Oahu. While I don't recall all of the specific details, the following is a pretty accurate reflection of the incident.

The client asked several questions, including "should our CEO make a statement about this? Should we put out a news release? Should we notify authorities?"

To answer those questions, I had to ask some questions.

"Has the oil come ashore?"

"No."

"Is it likely to?"

"Probably not in such quantities as to foul the beaches or affect tourism or anyone's health."

"Is the leak continuing?"

"No."

"Have you had problems like this in the past?"

"Not here."

My advice was to "First, notify all the appropriate authorities. Second, prepare, but don't issue, a statement. It doesn't seem justified based on what we know, but have it ready in case the situation worsens. Third, advise the CEO of the problem, but don't have him make any comment on it. Fourth, keep monitoring the situation and keep authorities apprised of any changes. And, finally, if you get any media calls, answer them honestly and then release your statement."

Little, if any, oil came ashore, and this was a crisis that didn't happen, but had it become one, the company was ready to swing into action. Not overplaying the incident was exactly the right move.

Once you have determined that you are indeed in a crisis situation, the next step is to activate the crisis response team. The CEO needs to follow this process closely to be sure that everything that should be done is being done. Each crisis team member should know his or her assignments in all types of crises and should be briefed on the status of the crisis.

Coordination of the team is the most critical aspect of the crisis. Everyone must work together and must also not work on elements outside of their areas of expertise. Legal and Operations should communicate and should be kept abreast of each other's actions, but legal should not be working on operations, and operations should not be making legal decisions.

What do you do if someone on the crisis team is out of the loop? Usually the person's top assistant will take the role during this crisis. Another option would be to have someone on the crisis team who used to work in that area handle this situation as well (maybe with someone else handling their usual area).

During a crisis, information comes from scores of directions, all at the same time. Some of it will be false, either through mistakes, assumptions, or genuine attempts at misdirection. Someone on the crisis team has to be responsible for the intake and filtering of information and the dissemination of it to the other members of the team. Someone else needs to be responsible for all media communication. These two must work together and with the rest of the team to make sure everyone has the same information at the same time and to determine whether that information has been verified.

The next step, almost always, is to prepare a media statement, which the CEO and chief legal officer should generally see before release. This is a brief statement that says that the company is on top of what has occurred and outlines what the current situation is and what is being done about it. The statement should include what you know and *only* what you know. At no time in a crisis should anyone speculate on anything; even something as innocuous sounding as "we expect the fire to be put out within the next hour" becomes something you'll wish you could take back if the fire is not put out that quickly.

Preparing a statement does not necessarily mean issuing it, as noted in the Hawaii example, but it's essential to have one ready.

One mistake that too many companies have made is to try to minimize a situation. The BP CEO did that when, early in the Deepwater Horizon incident, he said, "The Gulf of Mexico is a very big ocean. The amount of volume of oil and dispersant we are putting into it is tiny in relation to the total water volume." Shortly afterward, television newscasts were showing dramatic pictures of huge amounts of oil gushing from the bottom of the ocean. As the situation worsened and aerial photos showed a gigantic oil slick, his comment was repeated in the media over and over again, stirring anger and resentment.

In what form should the initial statement be released? Obviously, the text should quickly appear on the company's website and be dispatched to appropriate media. If it's serious enough, the statement should be delivered by the CEO at a news briefing. He or she should also take questions. While the CEO should stay on top of the situation, a public appearance will increase media coverage and attention to the incident. Where there is loss of life, an on-scene appearance will generally make sense.

A good example of CEO leadership in a crisis came from Mayor Rudolph Giuliani of New York in the wake of the 2001 bombing and destruction of the World Trade Center. In the hours following the attack, Giuliani held frequent briefings, with key public safety officials standing beside him, to update the situation and handle questions. His demeanor was calm but very serious. His answers were direct and honest.

In regard to how bad the death and destruction might ultimately be, he commented, "Too awful to contemplate."

That's not an answer anyone wanted to hear, but it was calming because those of us who lived and worked in the area knew that we were getting the honest truth. People are less inclined to panic and engage in harmful speculation when they feel certain that officials in the know are leveling with them.

What the Media Need

In a crisis, the media reasonably expect the following:

- Prompt response
- Appropriate executives ready to be interviewed
- Openness and candor
- An apology where appropriate
- Proof that the organization has been acting responsibly
- Prompt, effective corrective action
- Regular updates from spokespeople who have knowledge and authority

Let's look at each of those individually:

- **Prompt response.** In an active, changing situation, the media expect an organization to react quickly (as does the public) and update frequently. As I mentioned in the section about the initial statement, you need to say what you know when you become aware of the situation. Then the statement must be updated to reflect changing conditions.
- **Appropriate executives ready to be interviewed.** The media and public expect you to have someone who knows the crisis situation and is well versed in the operations and activities of your company. Offering a spokesperson who doesn't know what's going on or is told to hide important information is bad for both the media and you. The spokesperson must be someone with the appropriate title and responsibilities.
- **Openness and candor.** It is expected, and reasonably so, that you will be as forthright as you can. This doesn't mean that you reveal genuinely proprietary information, but it does mean that you outline what you are doing about the crisis, its current state, and how the crisis happened.
- **An apology where appropriate.** I have written about apologizing in Chapter 7, but as a quick recap, if something genuinely is your fault, you *must* apologize. This is the best way to begin restoring your reputation after a crisis. If it is not your fault, it's appropriate to express regret and offer sympathy or empathy to the victims.
- **Proof that the company has been acting responsibly.** You can't "brag," but if you have followed all regulations, had regular inspections, and acted appropriately all along, you should say so, and be ready to back it up. A blanket statement of "We act responsibly" or "Safety is our number one priority" is not enough. You must be willing and able to show your safety record, hiring policies, or whatever else will prove this.
- **Prompt, effective corrective action.** In other words, you have to be doing the right thing, not just something. The media and the public will not accept an answer of "we're assessing the situation and plan to do something when that assessment is completed." You need to be doing *something*, even while evaluating the situation. "We are still getting the scope of the whole situation; but we have already implemented our crisis plan, we are moving our employees and nearby residents to safety, and we are working with the fire department and hazmat crews to ensure everyone's safety."
- **A regular spokesperson contact who will have the latest information.** The media have the right to expect that the person updating them on the situation has the latest information and is the quickest and most reliable source of new developments.

Toyota, long-regarded as the most respected auto maker, lost its luster with some critical crisis-handling mistakes in 2009 and 2010 regarding safety defects in its cars. The poor decision-making began with not immediately disclosing problems that involved sticking accelerator pedals that caused the vehicles to speed out of control. It was only after several deaths in the United States were reported from runaway cars that the company went public, even though it had been trying to find and fix the problems behind the scenes in Europe.

When it finally decided to come forth and put an official on television to address the issues, it picked the wrong person. Toyota chose the head of sales for North America, James Lentz. While he performed capably in the interviews, his position was wrong. Any head of sales lacks credibility when it comes to addressing safety issues. The spokesperson should have been the president of North American operations or a top safety engineer with the company.

The safety problems and the subsequent mishandling of the issue resulted in Toyota's losing its position as the world's number one car maker.

Contrast that to what happened in December 2011, when the National Transportation Safety Board opened a defect investigation of the hybrid Chevrolet Volt after two of the vehicle's batteries had caught fire in crash simulations. General Motors CEO Dan Akerson quickly went public with print and television interviews. In a rare move for the auto industry, he announced that, while he was convinced the plug-in hybrid was safe, GM would buy back any Volts whose owners were concerned about fire risks. He also offered free loaner cars while the investigation was ongoing and offered to make changes in the battery pack if the government recommended them.

In this incident, Akerson set the standard for how a CEO should respond in a crisis situation. His bold and effective decision-making and his straightforward communication positioned GM as a responsible company that put safety as its top priority and was ready to stand behind its products. As a result, questions about the Volt's safety quickly died down.

What You Must Say in a Crisis

At all times during the crisis, the CEO—or anyone else who speaks for a company—needs to be prepared to answer these six questions:

1. What happened?
2. How did it happen?
3. What is the current situation?
4. Where did your system fail?
5. What was your initial response?
6. What is your long-term response?

However, if you don't know the answer to any one of them, the only appropriate answer is "I don't know." As I said before, during a crisis you *never* want to speculate, but you also don't want to leave your answer as "I don't know." Instead, you need to say, "I don't know, but we are working to find out," or "I don't know the specifics, but I do know that we were in compliance with all regulations in this matter."

A lot of people ask if the fourth question, "Where did your system fail," is fair. My answer is yes. In any true crisis your system has likely failed at some level. Did you build your plant in a low-lying area, only to find it flooded and destroyed years later, as recently happened in Thailand? Remember the definition of crisis we are using; if you face a situation that you should have anticipated and you cannot keep your operations going, that is a failure in your system. Similarly, if you find yourself in a situation you did not anticipate, that could also reflect a defect in the system. Even the most unexpected situation (Godzilla attacking) falls under the category of a natural disaster or act of war, and while your crisis plan may not have specific advice for being attacked by a giant radioactive lizard, you should have one for any disaster that threatens the well-being of your employees. Use that one.

Companies can also ask the media for help during a crisis. A CEO's or PR person's statement to employees or the public will invariably be used by the media. "We would like to ask everyone who lives in the area to refrain from using their tap water until we have word that everything is safe." "We are asking all employees on the late shift not to come in until we have secured the area." "Please do not call our offices for information; all of the information we gather will be immediately posted on our website."

The Forgotten Audience in a Crisis

When we conduct our crisis simulation training programs, the first task we give our clients is to create the communication portion of their crisis response plan. Most do a fantastic job: they list the steps they will take to communicate with appropriate government officials, the media, and a number of the steps they will take to deal with the crisis itself. However, almost without exception (and I've been doing this type of training for over 20 years), the team forgets to prepare communication for one group.

Their employees.

Too often, employees are overlooked in a crisis, yet communicating with them is vital.

Your employees are your ambassadors to the world. They also are an invaluable asset to your company. Ignoring them in a crisis can give the impression that they are not valued, and that will lead to higher turnover. Worse, it can create or increase their fears about their safety or the future of their employment. This is a time when the soothing presence of a CEO, in person or on in-house video, can do a lot to keep employees calm and loyal. Even if the CEO doesn't address the media or the general public in this kind of situation, an employee meeting or video can have great benefits.

What exactly do you say to your employees in a crisis? Precisely what you are saying to the media, plus what bears specifically on them but not necessarily the general public.

Internal and external communication must be in sync at all times, but especially in a crisis. Why? Because the external becomes the internal and vice versa. Now more than ever, things said to employees make their way to the general public, and employees have more access than ever to how the "outside world" is covering their situation.

One thing the company should immediately do is tell employees to refer all media inquiries to the appropriate corporate spokesperson. You can't stop them from speaking to the media, or blogging or tweeting, but you can encourage them not to. Explain that it is important for all of the information about this crisis to come from the person who knows the situation best, and that would be the corporate spokesperson. Misinformation from an employee or conflicting information can make a situation much, much worse. Most of your employees will genuinely want to help (unless they feel this crisis is something you should have been prepared for and prevented or that they are somehow being blamed), and you should explain that controlling who speaks to the media is important.

After the Crisis

Reputation restoration is a long, time-consuming, expensive proposition. There are companies that focus solely on this aspect of public relations. Once an image has been damaged, it takes a lot of work to get it back to where it was. Here again is where the CEO must be out in front, taking advantage of media and public speaking opportunities to restore faith in the company.

However, image restoration also represents a great opportunity. Some companies have emerged from a crisis with better reputations than they had going in. Others have used the crisis as the impetus for long-overdue changes to their structure, their products, and/or their management.

The most important parts of restoring your image after the crisis are taking and announcing steps to avoid a recurrence, reaching out to affected parties, being ready to compensate victims, and issuing sincere statements of apology, empathy, and contrition as appropriate.

Reputation restoration often means a change of policy and/or management. This is the direction BP seems to be taking in the aftermath of its crisis. It hired a new CEO, an American, and made its public relations effort more relevant. The new CEO is more open and empathetic—in all, a better communicator.

The company has spent millions on cleanup and has started sponsoring tourism ads encouraging people to vacation on the Gulf of Mexico.

Do crises create character? I don't think so. I think crises reveal character; they can say more about a company and its culture than a library full of books.

It is often said that crises make presidents. I feel the same is true of CEOs. Successful handling of a crisis shows a CEO to be a strong, effective leader who can bring proper resolution to the most difficult problems. This leader inspires confidence, and confidence affects stock prices. While no one wants to face a crisis, we know that all will; it's the handling of it that separates the top-level CEOs from everyone else.

Tips

- Identify potential crises now.
- Name your crisis team.
- Prepare a crisis plan.
- Update it periodically.
- Stage crisis simulation exercises.
- Be willing to talk to the media when disaster strikes, but prepare carefully before you speak.
- Don't forget to communicate with your employees.

CHAPTER 22

Hostile Takeovers: The Wolf at the Door

"You don't have to be the biggest to beat the biggest."
—H. Ross Perot, American businessman

We were finishing up a day of earnings call preparation in November 2002 when Robert S. Taubman, the CEO of Taubman Centers, Inc., asked me to step into his office and close the door. "Uh-oh," I thought. "I'm about to get sent packing, or at least criticized for some errant bit of advice." But that was not to be the case.

The shopping center leader showed me a letter from a competitor, Simon Property Group. The message was ominous: "Since you have rejected our friendly offer to buy your company, we will now initiate a hostile takeover bid."

Simon was the largest player in the shopping center field, owning and operating over 200 malls. Taubman, based in Bloomfield Hills, Michigan, was a small company, with less than two dozen centers, but with the highest reputation for quality in the industry.

It was truly David and Goliath. When David met Goliath in the Bible, David won. It doesn't usually work that way in modern day business, but it can.

Robert Taubman did not flinch. He told me, "We will fight. And I wanted to let you know that I will need a lot of your time to help us in this effort."

The battle was on.

It was obvious that communication would play a key role as the saga unfolded. A lot of people had to be convinced of a lot of things.

Most important, shareholders had to be persuaded that they would be better rewarded in the long term in sticking with the present management.

Key management personnel would need to be fully engaged and confident the battle could be won.

Other employees needed to keep working and not look for other jobs in fear that they might soon be out of work.

Even members of the Taubman family had to be persuaded that it was in their best long-term interest to stay the course and not accept the apparent bonanza that the offering price would bring. After all, it did represent a significant premium over the stock price.

Essential to success would be the ability of the CEO to keep his cool under fire and continue to express the optimism that was his trademark.

Many publicly held companies that began as family businesses end up being acquired in bitter squabbles that turn brother against sister and cousin against cousin. Dow Jones is a perfect example of a takeover battle that involved bitter disputes in the controlling Bancroft family and ended up with the company in the hands of Rupert Murdoch's News Corporation. Robert Taubman could not allow that to happen.

Facing a hostile takeover is perhaps the hardest thing for a CEO to handle. Pressure comes from every side and angle. You have to deal with legal considerations, financial considerations, internal relations, external relations, government relations, and operations.

Fighting Goliath

Obviously, fighting Simon's bid would be a long haul, with many players involved: corporate management, lawyers, bankers, merger and acquisition experts, public relations professionals, and assorted outside consultants.

Takeover battles are a gigantic chess game, and they can be chaotic. Robert Taubman would be bombarded by many voices, and his management skills would be severely tested as he decided which voices to listen to and what actions to take.

A seemingly endless series of meetings and conference calls followed. The CEO had to sort out a ton of analysis, advice, and recommendations, many of them contradictory. He had to listen to all parties, evaluate their recommendations, and come to firm decisions.

One of his first decisions was one of his wisest. He told his key employees, "I'll handle the takeover fight; you focus on the business. Your job is performance because our best defense is strong performance."

Your Employees during the Battle

It was critically important to keep employees informed and on board. The last thing a company under siege needs is an exodus of talent. So employees had to be reassured that Taubman Centers would win the fight and preserve their jobs.

It helped that Taubman Centers had been a good employer. It paid its people competitive wages and treated them well. It also enjoyed a reservoir of goodwill throughout the state of Michigan, which came to be a very important factor in the outcome of the battle.

The CEO pulled out all of the tools in his communication arsenal. There were emails, voicemails, and videos to communicate with employees who were located in 18 states across the country. He held Town Hall meetings, often speaking to large gatherings of employees. In addition, he said, "I literally would walk around the headquarters offices, trying to be as accessible as possible." The regular presence of a confident and friendly CEO reinforces the sense that things are going to be all right.

The strategy worked. There was no talent drain.

Communicating and the Legal Side

There was, however, a tough proxy fight, accompanied by legal battles. The Simon Group had offered $17.50 a share for the Taubman stock, a price well above what the stock was selling for at the time. Eventually, Simon and Westfield Property Group of Australia (the second largest company) joined forces and upped the bid to $20 a share, a more than 50 percent premium. Robert Taubman had to convince shareholders that the company would not only reach but significantly exceed the $20 level on its own.

The Taubman firm was started as a family business in 1950 by Robert's father, A. Alfred Taubman, a pioneer in the regional shopping mall industry. Even though the company had gone public in 1992, the family still controlled 31 percent of the shares. Thus, Robert was starting from a strong base.

But the matter was headed for the courts and the legislature. Simon sued Taubman, claiming the Michigan firm was acting illegally in the way they were voting their shares. After a series of confusing judicial decisions, the Michigan state legislature passed a law that validated Taubman's actions, thus ending Simon's legal threat.

Legislators are human beings, like anyone else. They respond to many things, but one thing that can influence them is how they and the public feel about the people involved in a particular issue. Taubman was a Michigan-based company; Simon was headquartered in Indiana. Taubman had been a very good corporate citizen over the years, with generous contributions to the University of Michigan, the Detroit Institute of the Arts, and many other of the state's beloved institutions.

Robert Taubman played the hometown card well in interviews and public statements, pointing out that "We had been responsible for more than two billion dollars' worth of investments in the state, and created 20,000 jobs. And what we were really saying is that if we stay here and continue to be an independent company, we will do more in this state and that will be positive for job creation and investments."

This effective communication of the Taubman company's value to the state and local area was instrumental in the favorable response of the public, the media, and the legislature.

After nearly a year, the costly and draining battle was over, and Taubman had won. Simon withdrew its offer, and as Robert S. Taubman had forecast, the stock eventually climbed to and well beyond the $20 offering price, eventually reaching more than three times that level.

There are many lessons in this David and Goliath story, but one is overriding: a company and its leaders need to communicate effectively with many constituents, and it has to start well before trouble strikes. Goodwill created now can be invaluable in the future.

Tips

- Communication plays a critical role when a company is under siege.
- Management cannot afford to lose focus on performance in such times.
- The CEO must be highly visible and express optimism.
- Ongoing communication with employees is essential to stability and staff retention.
- A history of good corporate citizenship and good employee policies can pay big dividends when a company most needs support.
- Good relations and good communication with legislators are critically important.

CHAPTER 23

Turnarounds: Righting the Ship

"There is nothing more difficult to take in hand, more perilous to conduct, or more uncertain in its success than to take the lead in the introduction of a new order of things."
—Jean-Jacques Rousseau, French philosopher and writer

Of all the challenges a business leader can face, engineering a turnaround is one of the hardest, but it is also one of the most rewarding.

One spring afternoon in 2006, Irene Rosenfeld was enjoying a relaxing drink with her husband at poolside at their home in Plano, Texas, when the phone rang. That phone call would change her life and transform one of the world's iconic companies.

On the other end of the line was Louis B. Camilleri, the chairman and CEO of Altria. Altria's Kraft Foods Company wasn't performing well, and Camilleri was looking for a new leader. Consequently, Rosenfeld would soon leave her high-level position at Frito Lay and become CEO of Kraft.

That began one of the greatest turnarounds in recent corporate history.

Rosenfeld didn't walk into the job blind. Due diligence convinced her that while reversing the company's downward trajectory would take a lot of time and effort, it could be done. Camilleri promised full support. His long-term objective was to spin off the food company from its tobacco parent, but he was not about to do so until Kraft's earnings and stock price could be brought back to a more acceptable level.

The "Plan to Have a Plan"

While Rosenfeld had worked for Kraft several years before, she obviously could not be fully abreast of its current situation. But shareholders, employees, and journalists are an impatient lot. As soon as she hit the ground at the company's Northfield, Illinois, headquarters, a torrent of questions began. "What changes are you going to make?" "Will many people lose their jobs?" "Will you sell off product lines?" And, most important, "What is your turnaround plan?"

Irene didn't have a plan. Yet. A long-term plan takes time, thought, research, and strategizing. So how do you satisfy and pacify anxious employees, shareholders, customers, and the news media when you don't know for sure what your plan will be? She needed to buy time to do the necessary groundwork.

So she outlined a "plan to have a plan."

The "plan to have a plan" worked like this: she would spend the next 90 days traveling around the company's facilities and the world talking and listening to stakeholders. She spoke with headquarters' executives, rank and file employees, sales personnel, retailers, consumers, country managers, and anybody else she could find who would give her insights on why the company was underperforming.

That bought her the time and confidence she needed from the many constituents to whom CEOs have to answer, including the board at Altria. It was the right move and it justified Camilleri's choice in bringing Rosenfeld on board.

During the process that summer and fall of 2006, she was able to keep questioners at bay by saying she was in the process of studying all aspects of Kraft's business and that the turnaround plan would be unveiled at an analysts' conference in Florida the following February. Meanwhile, she was quietly weeding out underperforming executives, upgrading product quality, revamping marketing, and making other "below the radar" changes in the company's structure that would enable her plan to succeed.

Communication skills are "make or break" in a turnaround situation. The first and most important audience that must be won is the employees. They have to believe that turnaround is possible and that this CEO can pull it off. Irene's personal appearances at Kraft locations around the world and her frequent description of Kraft as "a great company with great people and great products that is just underperforming" instilled a sense of optimism that this was a leader who could get it done.

She did. A year later, things had improved enough for the spinoff to take place. Five years later, the now-independent company was so successful and profitable that it could be split into two separate companies, both with bright futures.

Those who invested in Irene and Kraft were handsomely rewarded.

The Gillette Example

A few years earlier, another great turnaround had taken place in Boston under the leadership of a native Chicagoan, James M. Kilts. Kilts had successfully reversed the fortunes of another underperforming brand, Nabisco, after a successful earlier career at Kraft Foods. Thus, he was a logical choice to tackle the job of fixing yet another iconic company, Gillette.

His due diligence told Kilts that Gillette was fixable. It had great brands, was well-known and respected, and enjoyed market leadership in many of its categories. However, its earnings had been flat for five straight years, and its management had a history of painting an excessively optimistic picture to shareholders. He decided to take the job.

Arriving at Gillette's headquarters in Boston in 2001, Kilts says he found that while the company was constantly missing its targets, its executives were nevertheless complacent. "There was always a reason for bad results," he said, "bad luck or something. It took me a year to get the organization to realize that they weren't performing."

Kilts was aware of a key aspect of human nature: people make decisions on the basis of perceptions. His biggest initial challenge was to correct the perception that the company was doing "okay."

A few months after arrival, Kilts outlined a three-part strategic plan: "A financial turnaround, a strategic turnaround, and what we called functional excellence. After a year," he says, "people began to embrace those pillars and realize this was going to be an exercise to do things better, not finger pointing. We didn't want to place the blame on individuals. We had to make everybody feel they had ownership for the whole company."

In other words, challenge is a far better motivator than guilt or fear.

Managing expectations and showing momentum are two other key elements in engineering a turnaround.

In his first meeting with analysts as head of Gillette, Kilts encouraged tough questions and provided no-nonsense answers. He recalls, "John Manfredi [Gillette's head of communications] wanted to know why everybody hated it so much. I said, 'Well of course they're going to hate it; I told them everything was screwed up.'"

Kilts told Manfredi, "You'll see the attitude turn around as we get good results. And obviously, we got good results very quickly. All of a sudden, we were the darling of Wall Street."

This kind of candor is a hallmark of Jim Kilts and one of the major reasons that he was so highly trusted and respected by investors. He has always told it as it is.

Everybody—perhaps investors and employees most of all—needs a road map in a time of change. Having outlined the pillars on which Gillette's recovery would be built, the next step was to keep people informed of the company's progress. Each shareholder earnings call carried a theme line (you could call it a sound bite) that indicated how the rebuilding effort was going. As the numbers got better, the statement got stronger.

Initially, the sound bite line in the earnings call script and accompanying news release was "The turnaround has begun." A few quarters later, it became "The turnaround is gaining momentum." Next came "The turnaround is producing results." And, finally, "The turnaround is complete."

At that point, Gillette was sold to Procter & Gamble for $57 billion, a price that would have been unthinkable only four years before.

How They Did It

There are a number of common elements in these two success stories. The first is that the two CEOs entered the new arena projecting both determination and optimism. These are attitudes that quickly spread through the ranks.

They sought, and got, assurances from their boards of directors that they would be given the time and resources needed to get the job done.

They were candid from day 1 about how they viewed the organizations and their potential. Straight talk was the norm, and it built confidence in both internal and external audiences.

Instead of coming in with predetermined remedies for the companies, they started by asking questions, looking for strong points and weak points, and implementing policies based on what they learned.

Public statements were carefully chosen, and media appearances were generally limited. They were carefully focused on the work at hand.

They warned Wall Street not to expect a quick fix but assured investors that the job could and would be done in time.

It is unlikely that the turnarounds at Kraft and Gillette would have been so successful without the effective communication of these two dynamic CEOs and the outstanding public relations and investor relations staffs who assisted them.

Tips

- Due diligence is the first step for a CEO offered a turnaround position. The problems must be identifiable and fixable.
- Full support of the board of directors must be guaranteed.
- Realistic expectations must be set and communicated.
- Input should be sought from the many constituents involved.
- A plan must be clearly communicated to all.
- The public, and especially Wall Street, must be kept up to date on the progress of the turnaround.
- Communication with employees must reassure and also challenge.

CHAPTER 24

Government Hearings: Don't Be Nervous. Don't Be Flustered. Be Prepared.

"Testifying before Congress isn't a fair fight, and there are few rules to protect you."

— Charlie Cook, political analyst

It used to be said that you knew it was going to be a bad day when you arrived at the office to find Mike Wallace and the *60 Minutes* crew sitting on your doorstep.

Wallace died in April 2012 at the age of 93, but his memory remains strong with people who found themselves in the crosshairs of his aggressive interviewing techniques. It was never fun, and the executive usually came out on the losing end of the exchange.

But let me give another scenario, one that remains current: it's likely to be an even worse day when your assistant hands you a subpoena requiring you to testify at a Congressional hearing. This is especially true if the panel is investigating your company or industry. This could happen to the head of any company at any time.

I know of no more difficult or often unfair arena than a Congressional hearing, and nowhere is it more important to be thoroughly prepared and perform effectively.

Such hearings are sometimes more akin to theater than good government. With live, televised hearings and intense media coverage, they can give an obscure member of Congress a chance to posture and preen in the national spotlight.

A bad performance by the witness can bring global embarrassment and financial damage as it zips around the world through news telecasts and social media outlets. The head of a global corporation can no more afford to be seen in a bad light in Frankfurt or Sydney than he can in Washington.

A Grueling Ordeal

A witness can be required to sit and be bullied or berated for long periods of time without a break. Members of the committee can walk in and out of the room during the hearing, but the witness, often nervous and under oath, has to sit and endure whatever comes. One of my clients, whose company was accused of overcharging the government for defense purchases, once had to sit through an uninterrupted 2 hours and 45 minutes of such an inquisition.

Movie stars, or even small children, can be paraded before the gathering to say things that can make an executive's position look bad.

But executives are often their own enemies in these situations. They will drone through a prepared opening statement, eyes buried in the script, voice in a monotone. This is hardly the right start for someone claiming the propriety of his organization's actions or positions.

The opening statement is followed by a Q&A session for which the executive is sometimes unready, and he or she gives convoluted and unconvincing answers.

Don't these business leaders prepare for these sessions? Of course they do. But the preparation is often limited to rehearsals with lawyers focused only on what should and should not be said, neglecting some of the most basic aspects of communication.

Preparing for the Firing Line

The process can range from one day to several, depending on the difficulty of the situation and the scope and complexity of the issues.

Here's what such preparation should include:

- It must begin with the crafting of an opening statement that is written in clear, simple language and that directly addresses the major issues under discussion.
- Particular attention should be given to the most serious criticisms and challenges the speaker will face. Putting the company's position on the most negative issues on the record first gives the speaker a head start when the questioning begins.

- The participants need to study all letters or other documents received from the investigating committee to be certain that all areas that the committee wants covered are indeed covered in the testimony.
- The script must be thoroughly rehearsed, with video recording and playback, so that the speaker sounds confident and does not stumble over any words or phrases and can make frequent eye contact with the committee, especially on major points.
- All questions likely to be asked should be identified and answers prepared in the headline, elaborate, detail style outlined in Chapter 1.
- These questions and responses should be thoroughly rehearsed with video recording and playback to be certain that all answers are truthful, to the point, and well stated, and that good eye contact is maintained with members of the committee no matter how tough or unfair the question.
- The rehearsal questioning by the lawyers, the executive's communication coach, and government consultants should be at least as aggressive and challenging as the committee's questions are likely to be. This is no time to be timid or overly deferential to the leader.

The BP Example

The cost of inadequate preparation is high. BP's CEO, Tony Hayward, seemed particularly unprepared when he was called to testify in the wake of the deadly, and environmentally damaging, explosion and oil spill in the Gulf of Mexico.

Here is a portion of his Q&A session before the House Energy & Commerce Committee, with my notes on his mistakes and how he should have answered.

> ***Henry Waxman, D-CA:*** *Mr. Hayward, when you became CEO three years ago, you said that safety was going to be your top priority; you would focus on it like a laser. Your Website said, "safe and reliable operations are integral to BP's success." I want to ask you whether you think that BP met that commitment that you made when you became CEO?*
>
> ***Mr. Hayward.*** *Since I became CEO, we have made a lot of progress. We have made it very clear to everyone in the company that safe, reliable . . .*

(This answer is non-responsive. It is not surprising that Waxman, the committee chairman, was about to interrupt.)

> ***Waxman.*** *Have you met that commitment that you made?*
>
> ***Mr. Hayward.*** *And we made major changes. We made major changes to our . . .*
>
> *(Still unresponsive, putting the CEO badly on the defensive.)*
>
> ***Waxman.*** *You made major changes, but now we see this disaster in the gulf. Does that indicate that you didn't keep that commitment?*
>
> *(Still no direct response to the initial question.)*
>
> ***Mr. Hayward.*** *And one of the reasons that I am so distraught.*
>
> ***Waxman.*** *Could you answer yes or no? I don't want to know whether you are distraught. I want to know whether you think you have kept your commitment.*
>
> ***Mr. Hayward.*** *We have focused like a laser on safe and reliable operations, that is fact, every day.*

(Purely a boilerplate answer. He should have said yes, or, if he doesn't believe so, something like, "We have made an honest effort to do this, but we are not where I thought and hoped we would be.")

> ***Waxman.*** *Okay. Well, let me follow up on that. We had a hearing earlier this week with CEOs from the other oil companies. They were unanimous in their view that you made risky decisions that their companies would not have made. And in particular they criticize your decision to install a long, single string of casing from the top of the well to the bottom on April 19, the day before the blowout. They said this well design choice provided an unrestricted pathway for gas to travel up the well in the annulus space that surrounded the casing, and, of course, it blew out the seal.*
>
> *How do you respond to their criticism? Did BP make a . . . a fundamental misjudgment in selecting a single string of casing?*
>
> ***Mr. Hayward.*** *I wasn't involved in any of that decision-making.*

(Buck-passing never works before a tough questioner. The CEO should have an opinion on this. Hayward is now totally on the defensive and losing

credibility by the minute because of his failure to give direct answers to specific questions.)

Waxman. *Well, I want to know your view of it, now that you know about it, now that you know what your company did. Pursuant to your laser request that they be attuned to safety, do you think that that was a mistake?*

Mr. Hayward. *The original well design was to run a long string. It was approved by the MMS. There was only discussion in the course of the drilling of the well whether a long string or a 7-inch line that would be most appropriate. That is what I understand based on having looked at the documents and listened to our investigation team.*

The decision to run a long string, at least in part, was to do with the long-term integrity of well.

Waxman. *But let me be fair to you, because I am asking you to look with hindsight as to what happened and the decision that was made.*

But your own engineers warned in advance that this was a risky approach. And I would like to put on the screen what's called a planned review that your engineers prepared in mid-April warning against the long string of casing. As you can see, your engineers said that if you used a long string of casing, that it is unlikely to be a successful cement job. You would be unable to fulfill MMS regulations, and there would be an open annulus to the wellhead, and I have that on the screen.

Now, those are serious risks, a failed cement job, a violation of MMS safety regulations, an open pathway for gas to travel to the top of the well. The same document says that if you use the liner and tie-back approach, which is what Exxon Mobil and other companies said you should have used, you would have avoided or lessened these risks, and here is what the plan review said: If you used the liner, there would be less issue with landing it shallow. There would be a second barrier to gas in the annulus and a higher chance for a successful cement job.

Now, you said that BP is supposed to be focused like a laser on safety. Yet BP apparently overruled the warnings of its own engineers and chose the more dangerous option. How can you explain that decision by BP? Why were the safety recommendations of your own engineers ignored?

Mr. Hayward. *I wasn't involved in any of the decision-making. It's clear that there was some discussion amongst the engineering team, and an engineering judgment was taken.*

(Another direct and difficult question has been dodged—unsuccessfully. His preparation should have included thorough research on just what happened so he could testify credibly.)

Waxman. *It's clear to me that you don't want to answer our questions because isn't it true that you have served your life in BP? You have only recently become the CEO, but haven't you been in this business most of your professional life?*

Mr. Hayward. *I have been in this business 28 years.*

Waxman. *Twenty-eight years. So you should have some knowledge about these issues. And I sent you a letter in advance asking you—we were going to be asking these questions and to be prepared to answer it.*

(It is totally inexcusable not to be prepared to fully discuss everything in that letter.)

How can you explain this decision where you ignore . . . not you, yourself, but people who work for you who should have known that it was your directive to be a laser on safety. How could they have ignored these warnings from people right within your company?

Mr. Hayward. *There was clearly a discussion between the engineering team as to what was the most appropriate course of action to take. An engineering judgment was taken that involved long-term integrity . . .*

(Again, a stonewalling answer.)

Waxman. *It was more than an engineering judgment because April 15th there is a document, which is 5 days before the blowout, that said that using the safer liner will add an additional $7- to*

10-million to the completion cost. The same document calls it the single string of casing the best economic case for BP.

And the conclusion I draw from these documents is that BP used a more dangerous well design to save $7 million. What do you think about that? What is your response?

Mr. Hayward. *I believe that document also highlights that the long-term integrity of the well will be best served by a long string. The long string is not an unusual well design in the Gulf of Mexico. As I understand it . . .*

Waxman. *Say that again.*

Mr. Hayward. *The long string is not an unusual design in the Gulf of Mexico.*

(He failed to cite the frequency of use here and, if Waxman's upcoming 2 to 10 percent figure is accurate, this is a statement Hayward cannot support and thus should not have made.)

Waxman. *As I understand it from Halliburton's witness that was interviewed by our staff, that only 2 to 10 percent of those wells might use this particular string.*

Now, ExxonMobil and other CEOs said they wouldn't proceed this way. It appears to me that BP knowingly risked well failure to save a few million dollars. And even drilling 18,000 feet below the sea, if you make mistakes, the consequences of those would be catastrophic and, in fact, it turned out to be catastrophic. Don't you feel any sense of responsibility for these decisions?

Mr. Hayward. *I feel a great sense of responsibility for the accident. We need to allow . . .*

Waxman. *How about for the decisions that made the accident more likely?*

Mr. Hayward. *We need to determine what were the critical decisions and . . .*

(He should, and perhaps did, know full details of how the critical decisions were arrived at.)

Waxman. *Did you get my letter and did you review it?*

Mr. Hayward. *I have read your letter, Chairman.*

Waxman. *Do you realize in the letter that we asked you to be prepared to discuss these issues?*

Mr. Hayward. *As I said, I have seen the documents following your letter, and I cannot pass judgment on those decisions.*

(Now the Congressman is getting angry, and what follows will be even worse than what has gone before.)

Waxman. *Even though you have worked 28 years in the oil industry, you are the BP CEO, and you said like a laser you are going to . . . safety is the biggest issue and you have people under you making these kinds of decisions and now you are reviewing them.*

Do you disagree with the conclusion that this was riskier to use this particular well lining?

Mr. Hayward. *I am not prepared to draw conclusions about this accident until such time as the investigation is concluded.*

Waxman. *This* is *an investigation. That is what this committee is doing. It is an investigatory committee. And we expect you to cooperate with us. Are you failing to cooperate with other investigators as well? Because they are going to have a hard time reaching conclusions if you stonewall them, which is what we seem to be getting today.*

Mr. Hayward. *I am not stonewalling. I simply was not involved in the decision-making process. I have looked at the documents. And until the investigations are complete, both yours and others . . .*

Waxman. *That is somebody else's conclusion. What is your conclusion?*

Mr. Hayward. *I haven't drawn a conclusion, Mr. Chairman.*

Waxman. *I see. My time has expired and I am just amazed at this testimony, Mr. Hayward. You are not taking responsibility. You are kicking the can down the road and acting as if you had nothing to* *do with this company and nothing to do with its decisions. I find that irresponsible.*

This is an amazing example of either being unprepared for a hearing, deciding to stonewall, or both.

It wasn't long after these hearings that BP had a new CEO.

The McGwire Example

While lack of preparation and responsiveness was the cause of the BP leader's performance, former baseball homerun king Mark McGwire made a different mistake: preparation apparently based only on legal considerations. McGwire clearly stonewalled it in his Congressional testimony in March 2005 on the use of steroids in baseball.

Here was a man who was liked and respected by fans and teammates alike. He was one of the "good guys" of the game, but his reputation was badly tarnished by his amazing performance before the House Committee on Government Reform.

Here is a portion of it:

John Sweeney, R-NY: *It is rather an infamous occurrence that in the year you were breaking the home run record, a bottle of Andro was seen in your locker. My question to you is . . . your position now says that the use of that product, which is now illegal but was not then—how did you get to that point that was what you were using to prepare yourself to play? And if you could tell this committee how you ended up there. And I would like to know if other players have similar experiences. I think that would help us understand what you all live in.*

McGwire: *Well, sir, I'm not here to talk about the past. I'm here to talk about the positive and not the negative about this issue.*

Sweeney: *Were you ever counseled that precursors or designer steroids might have the same impact?*

McGwire: *I'm not here to talk about the past.*

Rep. Elijah Cummings, D-MD: *. . . Are you taking the fifth?*

McGwire: *I'm not here to discuss the past. I'm here to be positive about this subject.*

Cummings: *I'm trying to be positive, too. But just a few minutes ago, I watched you with tears—I need to ask a question. . . . I sit here and I almost got tears in my eyes watching you testify. And, you know, the thing that I'm curious about is, you know, it's one thing to say that we want to help. It's a whole another thing when those parents are sitting directly behind you and they wonder if this is real. I guess my question is you said something about your foundation and trying to help out. Tell us exactly what it is that you plan for your foundation to do.*

McGwire: *Well, right now?*

Cummings: *Talking about the future, as you said.*

McGwire: *My foundation helps out neglected and abused children. We have not talked about it, but I'm going to redirect about this subject.*

Cummings: *You are willing to be a national spokesman against steroids? We have all these high school kids that are emulating you and still look up to McGwire and others. And I think you said you are willing to be a national spokesman?*

McGwire: *I would be a great one.*

Cummings: *You would do it?*

McGwire: *Absolutely.*

Patrick McHenry, R-NC: *My follow-up question is to Mr. McGwire. You said you would like to be a spokesman on this issue. What is your message?*

McGwire: *My message is that steroids is bad. Don't do them. It's a bad message. And I'm here because of that. And I want to tell everybody that I will do everything I can, if you allow me, to turn this into a positive. There is so much negativity said out here. We need to start talking about positive things here.*

McHenry: *How do you know they're bad?*

McGwire: *Pardon me?*

McHenry: *Your message, coming from professional baseball, would you say that perhaps you have known people that have taken steroids, and you have seen ill effects on that, or would your message be that you have seen the direct effects of steroids?*

McGwire: *I have accepted, by my attorney's advice, not to comment on this issue.*

Rep. Dennis Kucinich, D-OH: *What can you say right now . . . to America's youth with respect to the use of steroids? Just in a half a minute to a minute.*

McGwire: *I would say that steroids are wrong. Do not take them. It gives you nothing but false hope. That's what I would say.*

Rep. William Lacy Clay, D-MO: *Mr. McGwire, we are both fathers of young children. Both my son and daughter love sports and they look up to stars like you. Can we look at those children with a straight face and tell them that great players like you played the game with honesty and integrity?*

McGwire: *Like I said earlier, I am not going to go in the past and talk about my past. I am here to make a positive influence on this.*

Clay: *Mr. McGwire, you have already acknowledged that you used certain supplements, including andro, as part of your training routine. In addition to andro, which was legal at the time that you used it—what other supplements did you use?*

McGwire: *I am not here to talk about the past.*

Clay: *Mr. McGwire, let me go back and ask you, would you have been able to perform at that level without using andros?*

McGwire: *I am not going to talk about the past.*

Rep. Christopher Shays, R-CT: *Never had the problem of seeing your colleagues use drugs?*

McGwire: *Pardon me?*

Shays: *Never had a problem of seeing your colleagues use drugs, steroids; is that what you mean? I don't know what you mean by you never had that problem.*

McGwire: *I am not going to get into the past.*

Those responses, directed by his lawyer, allowed him to avoid admitting what was generally considered to be obvious. He was off the hot seat for the moment, but his refusal to give straight answers sent a clear message: he had, in fact, cheated in an effort to break the home run record. His reputation was shattered, and his chances of ever getting back into baseball appeared slim.

It was an agony he had to live with for nearly five years, but then he did the right thing: he acted in a way that helped rebuild his public image and return to the game that had been his life.

After half a decade of virtual exile from baseball, in January 2010 he admitted in a television interview that he had, in fact, used steroids for 10 years as a player. He personally called Tony La Russa, his former manager; Bud Selig, the commissioner of Major League Baseball; and Pat Maris, the widow of Roger Maris, the player whose record he broke with his 70 home runs, and apologized to each.

McGwire said he had used both steroids and human growth hormone, not to get an advantage, but to reduce his injury rate. He added that he did not think it helped him hit home runs.

As this is written, he is the hitting coach for the St. Louis Cardinals, his former team, and the catcalls from opposing fans have subsided. It's a happy ending to a sad story, but it need not have been this bad. If he had testified openly and honestly, admitted that he made a mistake that he regretted, and apologized to all concerned, he would have emerged as a sympathetic—and still respected—figure.

The failure to consider the public relations aspect of that "no comment" testimony, meaning reputational damage, was devastating, and it reinforced a key lesson: it is folly to consider legal aspects alone in situations when a valued reputation is on the line.

"Winning" in the Hearing

It's hard to fully communicate the pressure that can accompany these and other types of hearings, including those before regulatory bodies such as the Food and Drug Administration. Body language is critical. A member of Congress even commented on this subject at the 2012 hearings about the collapse of MF Global, saying to the company's CFO, "I've been watching your body language and you seem like the odd man out. Do you realize how incredible your testimony sounds to this committee?"

It's very hard for a witness to come up with a persuasive answer to a comment like that.

Clearly, the young executive's nervous demeanor had affected the Congressman's impression on what was being said.

Many hearing situations are clearly not winnable for the executive or the company. But, even in the worst situations, a strong performance in the spotlight can have beneficial effects that include mitigating damage or influencing others.

In April 1994, a Congressional committee held hearings to consider tighter regulation of the tobacco industry. The hearings would be extensively televised—media interest was at a peak as health concerns about cigarettes worsened and critics of the industry became more active and powerful. Key portions of the testimony would be seen on television by millions of people in the United States and much of the world.

Many will still remember the picture of the heads of eight tobacco companies standing side-by-side, being sworn in before testifying. They were clearly under fire with hard positions to defend. Tobacco companies make products that, while legal, have serious health consequences, are now conceded to be addictive, and have no perceived benefits. The heads of the major U.S. tobacco companies were put under oath and given some of the toughest grillings I have ever seen.

Obviously, this was not going to be a good day for the controversial industry or its leaders, but for one tobacco company's CEO, at least, some good came from it. Thoroughly prepared, he presented his argument so effectively that his performance was the subject of a feature story in *The Wall Street Journal*, a prime source of news for investors.

This put his company in a more favorable light than its competitors in terms of the quality of its leadership, and it visibly increased the loyalty of the company's workers. Hundreds of them showed up late in the evening at a small-city airport to give him a rousing cheer when he stepped off the plane. So, while he probably could not and certainly did not win the day with the Congressional committee or, most likely, the television viewing public, he did convince major shareholders and the people who worked for the company that they had a strong and articulate leader.

As I said in the beginning, hearings of these types are very difficult, and a company or industry's chances of winning the day are not always great. However, with proper preparation and performance, the results can be better than they would otherwise be. To go in without adequate preparation is to invite bad media coverage and potentially damaging legislation.

It is too great a risk to take.

Tips

- Thorough preparation is essential to facing this difficult challenge.
- The opening statement must be well prepared and effectively delivered.
- All information requested by the inquiring body must be provided, and the information must be on the tip of the tongue of the person who is testifying.
- Both the opening statement and the Q&A portions should be thoroughly rehearsed and critiqued, with video recording and playback, prior to the hearing date.
- A strong, confident delivery and good eye contact are essential.
- A bad appearance can quickly go global and damage a company's fortunes around the world.

Epilogue

Are We There Yet? Good Leaders Know the Answer

"I don't think you're ever there. . . . You're always trying to get better."

— *Tiger Woods, American golfer*

It's not easy being a CEO. Anyone who has ever been there will tell you that, and anyone who is about to go there will find out soon enough.

The wise CEO hopeful devotes a lot of time to becoming the best communicator he or she can be, whether it's in one-on-one situations or involves large groups. The smart CEO keeps working on those skills and maintains a sharp edge.

Effective communication is essential to CEO success. It's almost staggering to look at how many constituencies a successful chief executive has to convince of something. The list includes those mentioned in the subtitle of this book: the public, shareholders, employees, and the media.

Let's look at some of the points we've made.

- Communication should be approached in a systematic way. The Scudder Method provides a model that can be successfully applied to nearly every communication situation.
- The best listeners tend to be the best leaders. Good listeners get the input needed to make the right decisions.
- Customs, culture, and language matter. Sensitivity to cultural differences is critical to success in a global economy, and so is the culture of a company. The CEO sets the cultural and ethical tone of the organization.

- The CEO needs a close relationship with the head of corporate communications and would be well advised to give that person C-level rank and access.
- Words matter. The wrong choice of words can be damaging to a leader's image and effectiveness.
- Apology, when appropriate, sets the stage for healing and moving forward. A CEO who can apologize has a distinct advantage over one who can't.
- All groups, especially investors and employees, are demanding more transparency than ever. Communication with them must be clear, concise, credible, and delivered with confidence.
- Employee loyalty is essential to growth and profitability. Most leaders need to do a better job communicating with the work force.
- The imperial CEO is dead. Today's CEO must have a productive partnership relationship with the board of directors and the work force.
- Dealing with the news media is part of a CEO's job and essential to promoting the corporate goals.
- Media training, with refreshers, is essential to success in the media.
- Public speaking is an important aspect of the CEO's efforts to show leadership and promote the company's goals.
- While anyone can become a strong public speaker through training and practice of the right techniques, most CEOs are not as good as they need to be.
- Taking questions after a speech builds a bridge between CEO speaker and audience and creates goodwill for the company.
- The speaker and speechwriter need to have a close relationship if the speechwriter is to fully capture the speaker's voice and ideas.
- Humor can be a great asset to a speech, relaxing both the speaker and the audience and making the experience more enjoyable.
- A leader's involvement in, and support of, philanthropy can benefit a company in many ways, but it's important to find the right cause or causes to support.
- A crisis is the supreme test of a leader's abilities, and every CEO will face a crisis at some point.
- Hostile takeovers are a common threat, but with the right strategies and execution, even a small takeover target can win.
- Turnarounds test the talents of the best leaders and require top-level communication skills.
- Government hearings may be the toughest arena for a CEO, but the one who prepares best will get the best results.

I hope you take several key messages from this book:

- Communication is at the heart of executive success, especially at the CEO level.
- Great communicators are made, not born. Anyone willing to work at it can become an outstanding communicator.
- Growth as a communicator is a never-ending process.

Tiger Woods is right: you're never really there. Staying on top can be as hard as getting there; it is a constant challenge.

Complacency can lead to the downfall of any leader, and that includes complacency in communication.

The techniques and practices mentioned in this book require constant renewal. Media and presentation skills need to be rehearsed and continually upgraded. Policies must be constantly reviewed and revised to respond to changing conditions. Evaluation of one's own performance needs to be ongoing.

I remember an old United Airlines commercial in which a coach is fiercely berating his football team in the locker room at halftime. "This guy missed a tackle, that guy dropped a pass, somebody else blew an assignment." The language was blistering.

Then, one of the players spoke up and said, "Wait a minute, coach. Aren't we ahead by 30 points?"

Scowling, the coach responded, "If you keep thinking like that, you'll never be a football team."

The best leaders of today don't rest on a 30-point lead. Neither do the leaders of tomorrow.

Tips

- Make ongoing development of your communication skills a top priority.
- Value and nurture relationships with all key constituents.
- Establish and maintain a solid reputation for yourself and your organization.
- Consider every communication exchange important.
- Take time to rehearse and practice.
- Listen, listen, listen.
- Don't ever sit on a 30-point lead.

About the Authors

Virgil Scudder has served as communication coach and counselor to heads of major corporations for over 30 years, serving clients in more than two dozen countries on five continents. He has headed his own firm, Virgil Scudder & Associates, since its founding in 1990, after leading the media training units of two of the world's largest public relations firms, Carl Byoir & Associates and Hill & Knowlton.

Prior to that, Scudder was an award-winning news broadcaster at major New York radio and television stations and networks, including WINS all-news radio, NBC News, and ABC News. During that period he also served for six years as a first-night Broadway drama critic, reviewing nearly 300 shows.

He frequently speaks and writes on communication issues and pens a column for each quarterly issue of *The Public Relations Strategist*, entitled "In the C-Suite." He resides in the New York City area. He can be reached at virgil@virgilscudder.com.

Ken Scudder is a writer and communication trainer and consultant. He cofounded Virgil Scudder & Associates in 1990 and, along with having bottom-line responsibility for the office, has conducted media, crisis, and presentation training programs in the U.S., Africa, and Europe. Ken has also written or rewritten speeches for industry leaders. He lives in Manhattan and can be reached at kenscudder@gmail.com.

Index